LIVING IN THE LAND OF THE DEAD

*An Anthology of Anthologies
of Faithful Fools Poetry
Edited by
University of San Francisco
Martín-Baró Scholars
(2014–2015)*

SAN FRANCISCO
2016

LIVING IN THE LAND OF THE DEAD
An Anthology of Anthologies

FREEDOM VOICES
P.O. Box 423115
San Francisco, CA 95142
www.freedomvoices.org
books@freedomvoices.org

© 2016 Freedom Voices and the individual creators.
All rights to poems remain with their authors.
No part of this book may be reproduced without written permission.

For more information contact:
Faithful Fools Ministries
234 Hyde Street
San Francisco, CA 94102

The front cover depicting the Faithful Fools' Court
was created by Ashleen Martinez.

The Tenderloin map and the street signs on the
chapter headings were drawn and designed by Nell Bayliss.

Layouts were produced by
the 2014–2015 Martín-Baró Scholars
at the University of San Francisco, a living-learning community at USF
devoted to community-engaged learning.

Tremendous thanks goes to Cathrin Jacob, who graciously took the lead
in layout work, long after class was dismissed.

Grateful acknowledgment is made to the many poets who were
interviewed during the production of this book.

Special thanks goes to Maya Nixon, who edited numerous interviews
with many poets whose work appears here in print.

Digital production services provided by Red Star Black Rose,
www.redstarblackrose.org.

ISBN: 978-0-915117-26-0
Printed in the United States of America

*Dedicated to Kay Jorgensen, who
continues to inspire and encourage many to faithfully
manifest our creative compassion through
acts of foolish openness, artistic regeneration,
and honest self-reflection.*

FAITHFUL FOOLS MISSION STATEMENT

We are called to a ministry of presence that acknowledges
each human's incredible worth.

Aware of our judgments,
we seek to meet people where they are through the arts,
education, advocacy, and accompaniment.

We participate in shattering myths about those living in
poverty, seeing the light, courage, intelligence, strength, and
creativity of the people we encounter.

We discover on the streets our common humanity
through which celebration, community, and healing occur.

Living in the Land of the Dead

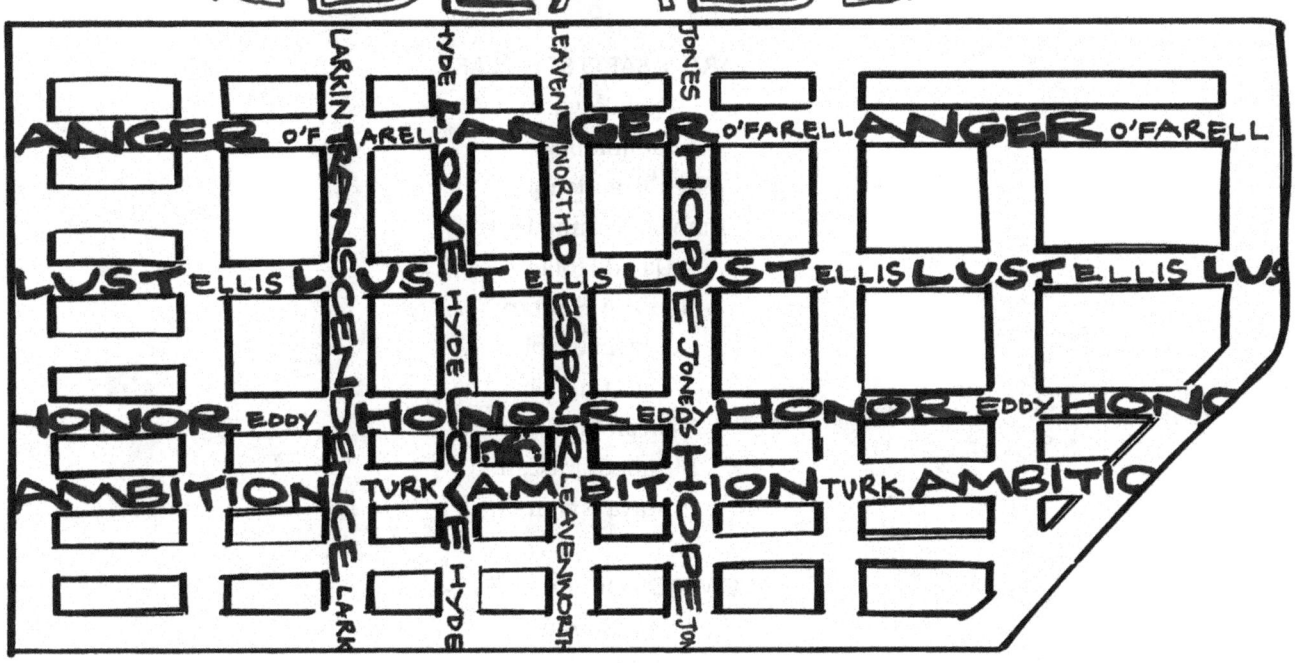

STEWARDS OF THE WORDS

FAITHFUL FOOLS
Carmen Barsody
Sam Dennison

MARTÍN-BARÓ SCHOLARS
Nell Bayliss
Kalmia Beets
Ben Brandenburg
Amber Jasmine Floyd
David Holler
Madison Houtary
Cathrin Jacob
Kara Knafelc
Ashleen Martinez
Elizabeth McCall
Maya Nixon

STEWARDS OF VOLUMES 1-5
RaMu Aki
Ed Bowers
Marsha Campbell
Ralph Dranow

EAGLE EYES
Kitty Costello
Mary Ganz
David Holler

LIVING IN THE LAND OF THE DEAD

NELL BAYLISS	-	Map
SAM DENNISON	i	Foreword
ED BOWERS	v	Introduction
CHAPTER ONE	1	**LUST AND ELLIS**
MARIE KAZALIA	2	Tender-loin
RANDY FINGLAND	3	noparent annie's exposure
PATRICIA WALKER	4	Days of Red
BOB BOOKER	6	So you want me to write you a poem ...
PHILIP T. NAILS	8	Birth Man
THOMAS CARNEY	10	In Rooms
ERIC ROBERTSON	11	The Prostitutes at Ellis & Hyde
CHAPTER TWO	13	**DESPAIR AND LEAVENWORTH**
GARY TURCHIN	14	Upon Hearing of Clive's *Suicide*
VLAD POGORELOV	15	Mosquitoes ...
KIRK LUMPKIN	18	Street Portrait: Two Versions Oakland, CA
DAVID ROBBINS	19	Alfie
GARLAND DAVIS	22	Old Can
MARY GANZ	23	An Urban Park at New Year
CHRIS TRIAN	24	Ash Wednesday
M.A. TUCKER	28	DA
KURT KUHWALD	29	A Call to Stillness
PAUL BELZ	30	Laguna Honda #1
EDWARD MYCUE	31	Dictionary of Conquest
VIANEY	32	What a wonderful day ...
DEBRA GRACE KHATTAB	34	she was sleeping

CARLA KANDINSKY	36	Put it on my tab.
BOB CLIFFORD	37	Gone
ALEX MILORADOVICH	38	Volcano Watch
ROBERT LAVETT SMITH	39	In This Deceptive Weather, for Valerie
NANCY WILSON	40	12/24/94
DAVID SHER	42	Tenderloin novice yearns for Dolores Park …
CHAPTER THREE	43	**ANGER AND O'FARRELL**
MARY RUDGE	44	Oh, the Millionaire/Billionaire CEO's
DANIEL MARLIN	45	Go Back Where You Came From
FORREST CURO	48	Untitled
DALE JENSEN	49	The Luxury of Well-Made Furniture
BERNARDO GONZALES	50	*Un Invierno en Nueva York*
	52	A Winter in New York
RENNON	54	Idolatic Power
KEITH SAVAGE	56	They are the Ones
RASHNA	57	LONELINESS
SUSAN KNUTSON	58	Three Days Retreat
JOHN RHODES	59	The Brut or *Le Difference*
GAIL FORD	60	Barely Divorced
BILL MERCER	62	Morning Falls
JULIA VINOGRAD	63	For Amandou Diallo, Killed by the NYPD
ALFRED TURI	64	Dedication Speech for the George W. Bush Sewage Plant
MICHELLE BINDHILL	65	Teardrop
ATLANTIS	66	be it ever so humble
CLYDE GALLAGHER	68	Plug
SARA THOMPSEN	69	Is it for Freedom

CHAPTER FOUR	71	**TRANSCENDENCE AND LARKIN**	
T. HAYES	72	Living In the Land of the Dead	
JUDY WELLS	74	Emergency Room Flashback	
MAREK BREIGER	75	Hayward April	
MOCONNOR	76	Lost to all the world	
DAVID T. MURPHY	77	Remember Surrounded	
AMUN VIA METU	78	I Have Become My True Self	
JOSHUA MANN	80	What I Am Learning	
MIKE NIEMCZYK	81	Voices	
JEFFERY MARLIN	85	Whiff	
YOLANDA WRIGHT	83	Why do I sit long ...	
MARY NORDKWELLE	84	I Saw a Man Today	
DEE ALLEN	86	Untitled	
RALPH DRANOW	88	Blindness	
MATT WOLF	89	together ... alone ... awake	
GARY BOLSTRIDGE	90	The Philosophical Forest	
ALEXANDRA LOONIN	92	Poetry	
OWEN DUNKLE	94	Out There	
MARTHA BOESING	95	The Visitor	
JESSE JAMES JOHNSON	98	Life Amoung the Gemini	
MITCHELL ZEFTEL	100	Henry David Thoreau	
CHAPTER FIVE	103	**AMBITION AND TURK**	
R. HOODLUM	104	Wanted in Land of Death	
RAMU AKI	105	Hyde Street O.G.s	
ETHAN DAVIDSON	108	Kala's Feast	
NORM MILSTEIN	110	The Wish	
WILLIAM BOWDEN	111	Direction	

MELISSA NEWMAN	112	Poor Playground
JOEL FALLON	113	Cockroach Dreams
GARRETT MURPHY	114	Return of the Dream Girl
H.D. MOE	116	Letters to Another Human Like Me
JOHN DELANEY	118	Mirror Buildings
DEBRA TURNER	119	It started...
UTAH CAROL	120	Tall Talk, Part Two
DIAMOND DAVE WHITTAKER	122	What Better Cover
JAN STECKEL	123	Bottle Pickers
KEITH WALKER	124	I Should Tell You About Desert Varnish
DON BRENNAN	125	Sun, Sun, Sun
ZACH KARNAZES	126	We Blame the Pirate
TAYLOR BROWN	128	Animal Limericks
VICKIE CIMPRICH	130	Dog, In Golden Gate
SANFORD DORBIN	131	Three Short Poems About Work
CHAPTER SIX	133	**HONOR AND EDDY**
JOHN DUKE	134	I Am a Street Performer
JACQUI	135	On the Street
JOJO	136	I am from a place ...
GLORIA RAINWATER	138	Gossip
MARSHA CAMPBELL	139	On the Death of Whitney Houston
JANELL MOON	140	Wheel of War
DELIA TOMINO NAKAYAMA	143	Poor Man on fhe Street
DEIRDRE EVANS	144	On the Shoulders of the Dead
FAY SMALL	145	Second Hand
ANNA SEARS	146	Lost Fathers
JACK HIRSCHMAN	147	Passover Scene: Civic Center, San Francisco

DENIS CALIN	148	Maw
TOM ODEGARD	149	Closer Than You Think ...
GEORGE WYNN	150	Back to the Street
O.D LUDYEH (BERNIE SULLIVAN)	152	Vision of The End
DAVE ROAMS	155	Why I Didn't Make the Russian River Trip
QRHANDJR	156	you get to walk

CHAPTER SEVEN — 159 — **LOVE AND HYDE**

WARREN	160	Weather
J. MICHAELS	161	Before Cats Walked
SHEPPARD BENET KOMINARS	162	The Talk About Grace
PAUL DRABKIN	165	The Heart of Things
DAVID SCHOOLEY	166	Flowers for an Old Man
RONALD F. SAUER	167	In the Metro
JESS (BEN) CLARKE	168	Trent
MEG WHITTAKER GREENE	171	Joaquin's Mind
JERRY RATCH	172	Brother Dream
ZACK REED	173	If nice guys finish last
JEFFERY JEWELLE JOSEPH JR.	174	Eternity
KAT KRIEGER	176	My Beloved Tenderloin
NORMAN DEPOVER	181	To All the Fools
RAY VALDEZ	182	Death and Resurrection
MELISSA MCNEIL	185	A Candle in a Glass
JAMES ZEALOUS	186	A Gift for All

CHAPTER EIGHT — 189 — **HOPE AND JONES**

CHARLES CURTIS BLACKWELL	190	Arise from the Broken
TONY TEPPER	191	You Choose War

ED BOWERS	192	Blue Tenderloin Kwazy Kat Zen
LYNETT DURGIN	194	We Come from the Sun
KATHRIN KAPP	196	You're not saying Billy has died …
DAN BRADY	198	In the Rain
VINCENT KOBELT	200	For the Blind Woman That Read Red
JEANNE BRYAN	201	July 30, 2007
MEL C. THOMPSON	202	Excerpt #43: From File Clerk at Allianz
J.R. JOHNSON	204	Ride the Tiger
MARK MORRIS	206	Fear
NAHSHON CHAPMAN	207	Poem for the Ministry
RICARDO LUNA	208	Mind the Pain
MARCUS COLASURDO	210	City Shaman
LOUISE SHULTZ	212	The First Day of Summer
MIKE STONE	214	Once upon an unlimited EBT card …
FRAN CESARONE	216	A Life on Purpose
JASON HY	217	Retired
DAVID PLUMB	218	News on A March Full Moon
BELLE STARR	220	The Day of Darkness
INDEX	222	

FOREWORD

Crossroads. This volume of poetry was born very near the corner of Turk and Hyde. You might call that intersection a crossroads. So too the intersections of Golden Gate and Jones, Leavenworth and Ellis, Market and Polk are crossroads. These literal places evoke a visceral sense of crossroads, where people of all kinds pass by one another, going about their business, just doing their lives. The people (and the grandeur of their dreams) at these Tenderloin crossroads are no less varied than those at any oasis on the ancient Silk Road that once connected the spices and exotic goods of the Far East with the awakening culture of Western Europe.

These poems originally appeared in five separate volumes, published over the course of 10 years by Will to Print Press, the publishing arm of Faithful Fools Street Ministry. Living in the Land of the Dead. That name for the series came from Ed Bowers, whose voice in person and on paper is rich and cutting and incisive. As a long-time resident of the Tenderloin, he knew whereof he spoke when he said that the Fools just had to get these poets published. He joined forces with Ralph Dranow, rAmu Aki, and Marsha Campbell to call on writers and artists to create slim but explosive volumes of creative words and images. When they were done with collecting, editing, laying out, and whispering words of magic so the creative force of these artists from all over the Bay Area could be given life on the printed page, the Fools held release parties where every poet would speak, sing, shout, and perform the work. Those readings were crossroads in themselves, transitory oases for celebrating life with vigorous words and heartbreaking truths.

These five volumes of art and poetry have circulated at many Fools' events—parties, readings, worship services, and art openings. Some are no longer available because the original files were lost, never to be retrieved. But we, Fools, have been determined to reissue these works in some fashion. It was in the spring of 2014 that we found the ideal partners to make this happen. We met David Holler and later Kara Knaflec, the co-faculty of the Martín-Baró Scholars (MBS) program at the University of San Francisco. Those scholars, it turns out, are freshmen who live and learn together. For an entire school year, they share a dorm floor and two classes, one in literature and one in rhetoric. Each year the MBS program joins with a community partner to relocate learning from the classroom to a neighborhood. Since Faithful Fools was founded as both a charitable and an educational institution and we knew that working with this project would be a very rich learning experience, we thought that the MBS students could meet the poets and editors, study their poems, and then create our Anthology of Anthologies. It only took a moment or two of conversation with David and Kara before we realized that this was a perfect match.

But here's the thing about crossroads, you always have a lot of choices of where to go. Such was the case with this project. Every step along the way held knotty problems. How to capture the feeling of the old volumes of Living in the Land of the Dead when we wouldn't be able to reproduce the artwork? How to bring the work together so that the poems read well? Could the work emerge without feeling forced or contrived? How to be true to the spirit of the original editors and writers?

The MBS students took their work seriously. They engaged in many hours of study, reading the poetry, talking with the poets, walking the Tenderloin, spending time with a wide variety of Fools. But the real effort became evident when they unveiled the plan for the book as a whole. "The poetry and the streets should come together," they said. "The poetry and the streets just fit together." So Nell Bayliss went to work creating a map that would help readers navigate the subtle connections among the poems and the place of the poetry. From the map grew the idea of cross streets identified by the visceral and the literal—Lust & Ellis, Despair & Leavenworth, and yes, even Transcendence & Larkin until we get to places like Hope & Jones . . . and our own street corner: Love & Hyde.

So this book is a crossroads, itself. A crossroads of people: A place where poets meet one another, where students meet poets, where faculty meet Fools. And a crossroads of life: A place where words meet the page, where truth meets dreams, where the past meets the present. It is an oasis on the long Silk Road of poetry that connects distant corners of the world. Along the way we realize that the travelers we meet are often rough and the experiences are rougher still, yet out of it all comes something remarkable, beautiful in all its complexities.

And now we come to the part of the story where we meet you, our readers. Once this book was curated and constructed, we went to our friends at Freedom Voices to publish it. Faithful Fools is really no longer a print shop and we knew we needed help. So we asked Kitty Costello and Jess Clarke to help us out. Then Cathrin Jacob, student editor from MBS, came back to finish what she had begun even though the class had ended more than three months earlier. This was not unexpected because each MBS student brought so much love and energy to the project; it is hard to describe how grateful we are to each of them. And so begins the list of people to whom we are so very grateful. We must begin with Ed Bowers and Ralph Dranow for that first volume, and rAmu Aki, whose friendship and intelligence have graced the Fools in more ways than we will ever be able to describe; Kay Jorgensen and Carmen Barsody for founding the Fools and being adventurers who welcome all who wish to come along for the ride. Of course, there are the other Fools, like Marsha Campbell who edited the third volume and Melissa Fafarman, whose proofing, editing, and (most importantly) encouragement are so graceful and inspiring; of course there is also Keith Walker, named as vision manager in the first volume, but really a Fool who inspires gentleness and creativity. We remember, too, the poets who are no longer with us in this world and thank them for leaving to us their words and visions. And of course the MBS students and faculty . . . brilliant work, I say to you, brilliant work. Thank you for helping us to see these poems with fresh eyes and renewed appreciation.

There are many other people to thank and acknowledge along the way and as is always the case with a project like this, the list risks becoming too long and unwieldy. The hardest of all is to find a way to acknowledge those whose names we don't know. They are here in their influence on each poet and on each student who worked on this anthology. But our deepest gratitude goes to the people who live in our neighborhood, those who sleep in the SROs and hotels, those who sleep on the streets, those who have lived here for decades, and those who have been here but a moment.

For all that we celebrate life with this text, we also remember that the Tenderloin is a hard place. Yes, vibrant, but let us not forget the deeply entrenched poverty of this place. Faithful Fools live very intentionally at these crossroads. We offer this Anthology of Anthologies, this record of Living in the Land of the Dead, as one way that we participate in shattering myths about those living in poverty, seeing the light, courage, intelligence, strength, and creativity of the people we encounter.

—Sam Dennison, a Faithful Fool

INTRODUCTION

Nobody moves to the Tenderloin of San Francisco unless the power of their presence and the intelligence of their words is not appreciated anywhere else.

When I first arrived here, it was not of my own choice. I had been married for eighteen years, and as my wife and I went separate ways, I had to find a place to live. North Beach was too expensive, so I found an affordable room with no kitchen and a bathroom in the hall. This refuge was located on 7th and Market.

It was a clean room, but in three years I have made it as dirty as the soil out of which wheat grows. Ripped up poems thrown onto the floor, Altoid ash tray cans overflowing with cigarettes, a cheap boom box playing old Charles Mingus recordings, a cold depression hanging in the air without advertisements for itself.

The first night I arrived here, I'd spent hours, which seemed like hundreds of years, standing on various San Francisco street corners with my ex-wife as she cried tears of regret that were as useless to me as I was to her now. Some con artist tried to sell her a computer.

Then, finally, she returned to her home, and I entered my room and tried to sleep alone.

But the words of the people on the street kept me awake.

All night long they sang to me.

You see, there is a Screaming Corner outside of where I live on 7th and Market. And by any other name it is called Pure Poetry.

The Screaming Corner is where those who love no one, and who no one loves, express themselves after 3:00 a.m.

"I wanna kill myself," was one line I heard repeated over and over again in a woman's loud and matter of fact monotone voice for over three hours.

Others on The Screaming Corner are not so discreet. They don't want to kill themselves.

They want to kill you.

But all of them have one thing in common. They have no face.

"I have to get out of here if it is the last thing I ever do," I told my ex-wife on the phone a few days later, sounding like an old rock song.

But I didn't believe I could.

Then I settled down. I went to the bars. I hung out on the streets. I made friends. I listened to people. I surrendered to God or the Devil or whatever operation runs the show. I started seeing the faces behind the words.

And I found out that it was here in the Tenderloin that I could express myself more than anyplace I'd ever lived in the United States of America. For over thirty years I had travelled and stopped in the East Coast, the South, and the West Coast, but now I'd finally arrived.

The Tenderloin is beyond all coasts. It is the last stop.

The end of the road.

But endings can be good. The entertainment industry depends on happy endings for movies and plays. However, most of them are false.

The endings here are real. In three years, I can't count the number of people who are now dead, or the amount of angels who have helped me survive.

I only hang out with literary types South of Market a few times a month, but The Screaming Corner in The Land of the Tenderloin Dead is where visceral poetry, and love and hate, are honestly expressed.

Words here are live wires inserted into your brain in the middle of the night when you look out your window to see the waning Moon.

These words will make and keep you awake.

These words are mantras that you will never forget if you have the courage to take them seriously.

Welcome to Living in the Land of the Dead and the Tenderloin Anthology of Poets and Writers.

Let The Screaming Corner of this anthology enter your soul, and and like me, you may be saved.

Read carefully and respect what is written here, and I humbly pray these stories and poems inspire you to survive under all circumstances so that you can go on to help someone else to do the same.

Read slow.

Slow is best.

Fast is a mistake. I can attest to that from a lot of people I've known in this zone whose split decisions ended badly.

Slow it down so slow you can see it clearly coming toward you and not panic and get into a wreck.

The highway to the Land of the Dead is merciless and allows for few mistakes.

Do not drive off the road.

See the faces of those driving toward you and show respect.

Understand this book. Living in the Land of the Dead contains road maps, accident reports, and prayers.

This document is filled with human life crying like a helpless baby, or the blast of a lonely horn, or the desperate reaching out to others who are too late to be saved.

And in the dark moments of your life, when tears force you to be honest with yourself, these words, written down and solidified, will help you to accept that you and everyone you ever hated or loved are all in the same boat.

Naked or clothed, blessed or damned, full of joy or despair, we of the Tenderloin are represented in this book whose intent is to give the people on The Screaming Corner a face that can truly communicate with dignity to others.

—*Ed Bowers, a Faithful Fool and Tenderloin Poet*

Chapter 1

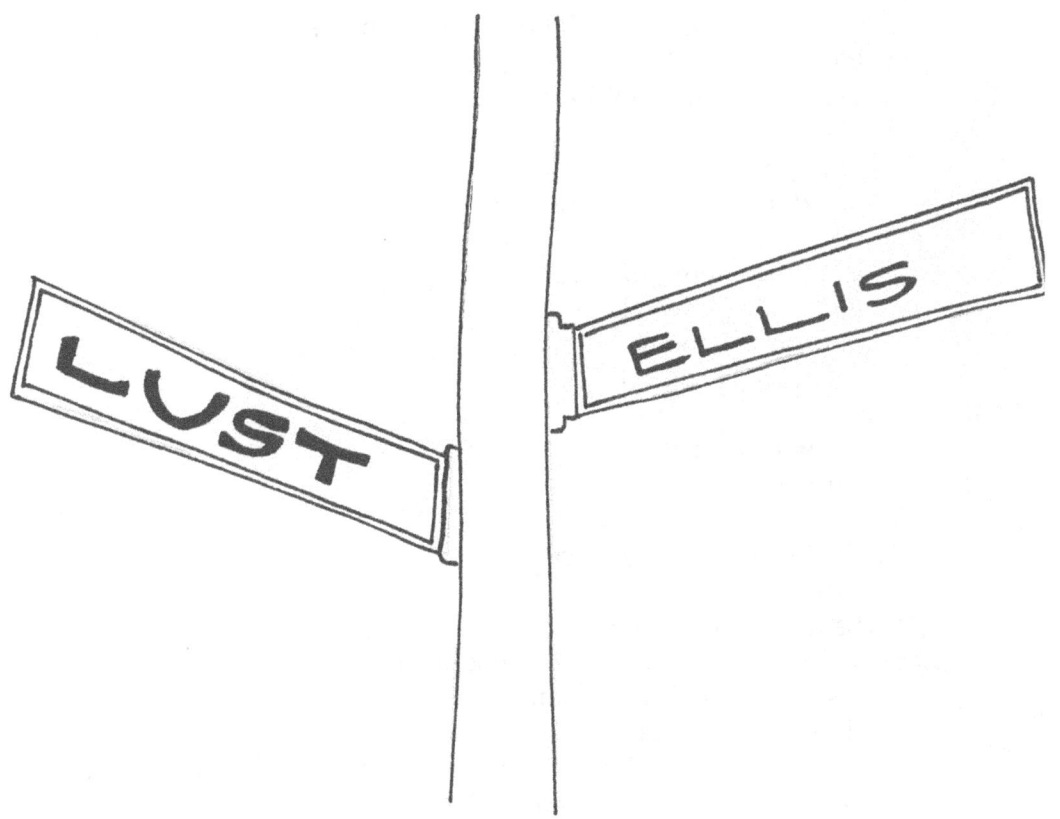

Tender-loin

Marie Kazalia

    statuesque women with hormone pill breasts
    low tops
    mini skirts atop LONG legs
    big feet in size 16 pumps
    hair grown long
    or extensions woven in—
    wigs usually blonde
    affecting a feminine walk
    up & down sidewalks
    noticed one today
    her scared & pitted face
    even more
    out late at night
    early morning
    trying to get tricks
    getting into strangers' cars

    Selina told me her ribs hurt
    where some guy got mad & punched her
    saying "you're NO woman"
    threatening to stab her with a knife
    went to his parked car looking for something
    came back as she stood on the dark sidewalk
    but never saw a knife
    "fucking weird-o-s out there" she says
    really high—
    doing a lot of talking

noparent annie's exposure

RANDY FINGLAND

they called her
a knockout
but it was
her beauty
they spoke of

because she
was gentler
than a mid-
summer night's
breeze everyone
wants more of

even on
the streets, much
meaner than
the cruelest
wind that brings
winter's too
harsh weather

and for her
made sure
she'd never
awake to warm
up in
the thawing sun
of spring

Days of Red

Patricia Walker

Running from the IRS
No reason, place, or thing
Not to confirm appointments of my contemplation
Hillary or Obama
Which way is best?
Only thoughts of meat, no house this time
"No, I do not read the newspaper"
Red Meat for a Scarlet Lady
A lady of culture, for all to read about
Flowers running allegedly to please my hardware
Can you read?
Fashions my best news for a Lady of Red
No dress, no flowers, no polka dots
Just read me my rights
I'm running from the IRS

Remember, just running for that Red Dress so beautiful
No more Woman in Red, too much sex, not enough food for
Thought
Just dig right in, the world's strawberry, so dead after the show
Dig that grave for all who shopped in Discount Fabrics,
Discount Shoes, Discount Food
Not for sale for the Lady for her fate
Her fake fur red coat, and not only did we all notice the Red Skins
Foot fashion, football red stains on your cherry tree

Which way to the top
Man in red, he is dead
Play for money, for your Scarlet Lady
Hand me your binoculars, I think we can see her now
Only thoughts of meat, tomgirls only eat
Hard up for a dress, Scarlet Lady
These are hard times for my fashion flare
Running for office, from the IRS, and looking for my red fake fur
So hard up one starts to feel dead by night, football by day

Looking for that red dress, and unconditional love
No strings attached, No, if you're white you're right
Red
Never to live, forever only
Titles
Never to live, forever only
Money
Never to live, forever only
Famous
Never to live until a lady arrives wearing the red dress of all her
Dreams, satin
Fashion

So you want me to write you a poem …

Bob Booker

So you want me to write you a poem
Like Bukowski would write?
Something like
"moths go batty trying to put on the eyes
of light bulbs in artificial cities,"

Or something like
"the windows screamed like doves
 after the bombing of Milan,"

Or even something like
"sleeping with the whore of your fancy wife
you must someday die like I have lived,"
Something like Bukowski would write;

Something with a little black French lace
On a hot, summer night in L.A.
That smells like a cheap Macy's perfume on sale,

Or something that sells like the sexiest sushi
Or the hottest salsa in town,
Something like Bukowski would write;

Something like an old Army knife
That bleeds too many B-movies,
That still laughs at all the dumb, blond
Beauty in Hollywood,

Or something that never weeps
For the already dead and buried,
Something like Bukowski would write;

Something a little crazy, used up and wise
That still shakes the same crooked dice
For the same broken window tomorrows,

Still betting on the same losing horses
At the same lousy track shouting
"Isn't life grand?"
At the same closed pay window;
Something like Bukowski would write.

Birth Man

Philip T. Nails

Happy nail day birth man.
Here is a kaleidoscope
for the strip club.
Enjoy breasts spiraling
into the eye you were given
by the explosion of cells
in your mamma's belly.
Give yourself dreams by
tickling tattoos lining your
thighs running out Turk
in solid belief that
there is an Ocean if
you run far enough.

Too bad you can't drink
salt water or breathe like
dolphins singing tide hymns.

Birth man runs drunkenly
up and onto a beached whale
lying dead and graffiti ridden
after seeing Whale Rider the film.
In his search for infamous carcass
he comes across band of smoking
gypsies making out like sirens
in fog moving thickly
blinding amateur scientists
and curious writers.

Reflect on this present moment
that unfolds through breath.

The smile muscle.
Use it or lose it.

I am not far away from
him, you or him.
He is never far from us
and they are always us
if given enough time.

I've eleven years of the loin
inside me. It lives against spine
forever leaking acid I then shake
from a razor.

In Rooms

Thomas Carney

Lovers return their gifts/on fire
Are underhanded minds worthy of all
These wasteful thoughts
On a trip under the ground
Of my past home/on fire
Is my welcome/is my return
In all these empty arms

In order to live/in order to survive
In order to get by
There are some days
I empty my arms

Is all I see/the fruit of this world
Belittled with the poison of media infections
Is what I hear all these nights
A danger dance with sorrow

It's cold inside this aging flag
Ignoring the hints of this chilling wind
There are some days I cancel all sounds
Empty my eyes
Then
I may care
To give
One more day
a chance

The Prostitutes at Ellis & Hyde

Eric Robertson

Some of these women move like
wildebeests on a dry Saharan plain
weeks thirsty for water
clouds of dust blown up around
ankles strapped to high wooden heels.

I saw one run mad today
snorting and guffawing
chasing a car
begging for something to fill her veins
caught with a case from the tsetse fly
the rabid tail biting sickness
no clothes beneath her coat.

The women here are like wildebeests
on a dry Saharan plain.

I watch their lumbering butts
the big ones
full of meat
the ones all used up
one heel broken
flopped over a car
bent over
hair touching the street.
Male lions on the prowl

Vietnamese children running
laughing
weaving in between.

Chapter 2

Upon Hearing of Clive's *Suicide*

Gary Turchin

I do not pretend to understand the mind of God
any God
any mind
even my own.
How then are we to understand
a child's mind?
Even our own child's mind
our own precious child's mind?
It's an infinite mountain we climb
on finite feet
one step after another
one plateau
a base
to the next rise.
The valleys make reservoirs of our grief.

Mosquitoes ...

Vlad Pogorelov

Mosquitoes,
Cockroaches, and
Spiders
My lovely roommates
And my only true friends
I love you
I love you
I love you
In a sick kind of love
Which will make an executioner happy
And the victim will suffer no more
Only pleasure from the torture
And the pain has no right to exist

And some time my eyes are
Staring at you: big, lonely spider
You are sitting in the darkest corner
Of your dusty net
Waiting for me to get in

And I know for sure
That a giant mosquito
Made his home
Inside my swollen heart
There is plenty of blood
Inside those chambers

And when I can't hear you clearly,

When you are talking to me on the phone
I feel that a cockroach is moving
Inside of my ear

And sometimes I feel
That there is nothing to feel anymore
Ever since my soul was amputated
And smuggled to India
By a gynecologist
Who was seeing my mother
Long time ago, before I was born

So,
Mosquitoes,
Cockroaches,
and Spiders
You are my only friends
Who are sharing my soulless fate,
Abandoned by lovers,
Forgotten by long time friends,
Forsaken by my motherland and the ancient gods
I am living a sheltered life
As a derelict

And it seems like it's time
To jump into the water of a substance
Which looks like a residential street
Or a boiling sea
Depends on the point of view
Or the angle of the mind
Or just walk out the door
And swim to the store …
Buy some cheap liquor …
Go back home …

To this slow SINKING ship
And to share my fate
With my only true friends
With my only true love
With Mosquitoes,
     Cockroaches,
      and Spiders
'Cause I am a derelict
And I am living a sheltered life

Street Portrait:
Two Versions Oakland, CA

KIRK LUMPKIN

I.

Hat brim
    shadowing his face
       from the corner street light
Trying to look
    sinister
    in the pose
    of a child soldier thug
But
    unbeknownst to himself
Peeking out
    from behind his eyes
Is the bruised and frightened soul
    of an angel

II.

In the hat brim shadow of the street light
Just a-hangin' out on the street at night
In the pose of a child soldier thug
Lookin' like he might be dealin' some drugs
Like he might be packin' a pistol
But in his eyes bruised soul of angel
In his eyes bruised soul of angel
But in his eyes bruised soul of angel

Alfie

David Robbins

"Ya know the men's room
at the Lakeview Library?
Well, I found a *Chron* in there
This morning." *"A what?"*
"Yer *deaf and dumb,*
Right?" *"A what?"*
"A Chron-i-*cull.*
It's a news-*paperrr?"*
"Oh." "Found a copy
in the *men's room,*
and I saw my brother's name
in the obituaries—
My brother *Wilber ... See?"*
"That's your *brother?"*
"Prostate Cancer.
Lasted *eight* years.
Used to stop by here
To chat, like you do.
When he stopped comin'
I knew he was *done for."*
"It says there's a service
this Sunday. Are ya goin'?"
"Yer *kiddin*! What're you doin'
fer *brains*, kiddo?
A private residence in
San Bruno? Oh yeah,
They'd just love to see
This smelly old carcass

Stinkin' up those nice
Front row seats! Yer
Goin' *brain dead,* right?"
"But you're his *brother—!*"
"Willie's the oldest
I'm the next to the youngest
And I'm the next to go."
"O no you aren't."
"O yes I am.
One more winter on the street
and I'll *kick off.*"
"So why not use your government
checks for a *room*
instead of all those cigarettes?"
"I can't stop *smoking*! Besides,
The cigar store'll go outa business
And *Sue* would lose her job…
Look at all those filthy pigeons *eat!*
The little *thieves!* Bird seed
Costs me a *buck a day,*
And that *adds up,* kiddo! …
I bet they're burning
Willie up *right now.*
I've decided to leave my body
To the UC Medical Center.
Prob'ly they'll cut me up
And throw me down the toilet.
I even said that to the doc,
And he says, 'No we won't!
We'll say a *prayer*
While we dump you down the toilet!'
Funny Guy!
Reminds me of
Humphrey Bogart.

Says I'm in trouble
For *twenty reasons,*
None of 'em *pleasant ...*
So waddya *think,* kiddo—
What's on the other side?"
"I think it's a mystery, Alfie."
"What'll all these pigeons do
Without *me* feedin' them? I bet
They'll miss me, the little thieves!
You'll worry too about the other side
When your time comes ...
We're all the same, kiddo.
When you get right down to it,
We're all scared of the dark."

Old Can

GARLAND DAVIS

I found a can
without a tag
And wondered what I had

I pictured yams,
beans with wax,
or maybe Popeye's spinach

Sadly, I couldn't see
Why I should keep it
The black eyed peas couldn't see either

An Urban Park at New Year

Mary Ganz

Remember the brown of the grass?
It is the place where old men gathered.

Nearby, buildings issue up inside the scaffolds,
Golden faces slatted into burnished wood.

Dogs haunt the edges, memories of crust.
We build a shrine upon the windswept bench.

Are we to sacrifice our laughter,
our little joke, playing in the shopping carts.

We lift dry earth by shovelful,
then let it fall. Fences rise around us.

The Sower scatters shards in autumn light.
I run my fingers deep in warrior marks.

Just what do I yearn for in this life?
Surely g-d has put these numbers on my list.

Ash Wednesday

Chris Trian

I mark my forehead
with the ashes of the burning world,
with the ashes of the burning people
who are dying of our burning soul.
And it is *our* soul.
The living too are on fire.
Our ashes are mixed together
in the crematorium of history
for this unnecessary
Sacrifice.

I anoint my forehead
with the sign of a crucified planet.
Like a third eye,
it sees in the darkness.
Million, billion of victims
put to death
for thinking,
as though God gave us not
our brains and wills.
As though it was a crime
to be human and to doubt
the status quo of the law.

I mark my brow
with a new law,
a communion of sinners
not just saints;

the sign of the cross
like any two crossed streets
on any intersection in America.
Intersection of hope and fear.
Intersection of survival and death.
Intersection where
the darkness meets the darkness
and the light kisses the light.

Something is opened and
something is held up like a heart
between the eyes
crying like a newborn child.
The child is hope.
The ashes are the past.
The mark on my forehead
is a scarecrow burned
and pierced with arrows,
signaling to the sisters and brothers
who find themselves with
nowhere to sleep.
And though many have homes,
there is still nowhere to sleep
in America this Ash Wednesday.

I mark my forehead
with the ashes
of the phoenix.
The phoenix is the citizenry of the world.
It rises awkwardly like a bumblebee
on wings too small for its great bulk.
Ten billion people's worth of bulk, or is it bigger?

Soon there will be more people than

there are stars.
The stars too are homeless
and the black holes
are ash marks on the forehead
of God.
Everything mourns
for this wrong direction
time has taken,
which only space can save.
Not the space on the streets
or in The Inn,
but the space in the heart
where all the burning buildings
gather, people leaping from their roofs.

It is not the fault
of politics or politicians only.
They will have their reward.
It is the fault
of the loss of our memory
that we were CONNECTED once.
That WE are the Holy Grail
of immortality.
That we are ONE FLESH.
That the ashen cross
was once a living tree
with ten billion leaves.
That we are that tree of life.
That the fire is not a holocaust
but a Holy Cost.
And that cost is simple.
That we see ourselves
in the faces of those
whose ashes we wear

whose faces we see
tied to the crossroads of everywhere.

There is no time
to wait for a savior.
We must BE that savior,
or go in sackcloth and ashes
backward into dinosaurs,
because she dances
to a different drummer,
who knows nothing
of Wednesdays or ashes.

A planet who still remembers
how to dance on the point
even if her children
have fallen.

Because a new plague is upon us.
Its name is ignorance and denial.

And no flower's scent
can mask its death.
"Ring around the rosies.
Pocket full of posies.
Ashes, ashes,
We all fall down."
Or maybe not.
The choice must be made
TODAY!

DA

M.A. Tucker

Paper chasing
           Clouds erasing
Seems I'll never
           Be as clever
As the lady
           Who's so shady
Lookin' for blood
           After the flood
Nothing but rocks
           And broken down clocks
Guess I'll just ride
           To find my pride
I know now it's lost
           Under the frost
Why sac~ri~fice
           At this high a price?
Just to feel good
           The way I Should

A Call to Stillness

Kurt Kuhwald

Like bird wings, perfectly balancing the sparrow's lion heart
Like lungs drawing into the body the precious fluids of air, then ...
    exhaling, releasing the mind along the tunnels of nostrils
                      the great cavern of the throat.

The end of paralysis: Keep moving.

Keep moving, I said, as I packed and boxed, sorted and discarded
                in my old, dying life ... *Keep moving* like wings,
        700 feet above the coastal California hills.

Keep moving ... and the city took form through the fog
        the city of fists, the city of dark exhalations.

Keep moving ... and the fog, wet and thick, gave up its clinging
            and the city of open hands and lungs filled ...
                      Like a beginner, once again.

Keep moving ... without command
            or should.

Keep moving ... with the bare attention
            the sparrow pays to wings steady and true
                Cutting the air with the courage of each breath

Keep moving ...

Laguna Honda #1
for Mitchell Zeftel

PAUL BELZ

Poems hide out on this ward.
Blankets, wheel chairs and beds shelter them.
Patients sleep at 6 PM.
One guy has a puffy face
Like a biscuit or a slice of vanilla cake.
Another grows pipe cleaner thin legs
That confine him to his mattress.
A third's arms are tattooed with needle holes.
All sleep, shifting and uncovered on their beds.

TVs buzz and flash numb light their way.
One set reports the weather to a man stuck inside.
A second's turned on Sesame Street,
Elmo the monster's lonesome.
The next one's on a cooking show—sirloin cubes
Sizzle with portabellos and brandy.
No one here cares. It's 6PM, life is short,
Everyone sleeps. But poems hide out here.

They creep away from wheelchairs and beds,
Sneak from beneath blankets. They wander
Onto sleepers' faces and gently dig
Down into their minds. They'll drift around
Like wind borne pollen to fertilize dreams.

Dictionary of Conquest
It's All Paranoia Until it Happens to You

Edward Mycue

Judgment of peers
foundation notice martial law emergency
    influx of

single-bid detention camps
undisclosed locations

railcars reportedly equipped with shackles

a Homeland Security plan entitled
    ENDGAME its
goal the removal of "all removable aliens"

"potential terrorists"

construction & refurbishment
of detention facilities

housing perhaps millions of people
indefinite imprisonment of anyone

who donates money to a charity that
turns up on a list of "terrorists"

organizations or speaks against the
government's policies

What a wonderful day …

Vianey

What a wonderful day
Out my window 4th floor.
My eyes seem to stray
at the cars, galore.
I look forward to saying hi
To the people on the streets.
But I just can't get by
Remembering the heats.
I refer to the heated confrontation
With the cops.
The man sells clothing to a nation
At the top.
He minds his own business and has goods displayed.
The dollar t-shirts,
good although frayed.
Violently, the constable of "peace"
threw his merchandise in the unit.
There is no wind between the trees,
his eyes are just swollen.
Now, I wonder,
Is the street merchant really a threat to you?
I donated some clothes to him and shoes.
Cuz I'll tell you, straight up,
The Kidnapper Lieutenant scares the hell out of me.
Imagine what fear the 19-year-old did see.
So why criminalize the brotha who is trying to contrive?
The peoples of 'Loin, We Will Survive.
Brutalities of police,

I see it all the time.
Homeless, the ill, disenfranchised …
know my rhyme?
Unfortunately you do and all aligns.
So next time you see the cab sign about homeless,
Which instructs you NOT to give
Just hope misfortune does not knock on your door.
Make it tough to live.
And just because you or I live on the 4th floor
Does not mean others are okay to be ignored.
Whether you like it or not,
We are all entitled to be.
My politics can't be bought.
I am you. You are me.

she was sleeping
for Maria King

DEBRA GRACE KHATTAB

she was sleeping
when they saw her
her true face turned inward
to face the fright of desperate dreams
dreams of understanding lost histories
dreams of a long unknown home
to lay her head down in
and once again
I felt the thin line of cloth
between the concrete
and my own desires
for sleep, sustenance and safety
because she was sleeping
as I tried to
when the cold bit at me
at every exposed finger
at my reddening cheeks
biting and chewing up the hope for sleep
but she managed to sleep
until they saw her
and their feet lashed out
because they could
and their fists struck out
because they wanted to
those two teenagers
whose loud voices
dragged her nightmares out of her head
whose hard hands

finally silenced her schizoid voices
whose footprints decorated her skull
until all her dreams split open and out
to spill into her blood on the sidewalk
and you know what? dreams die
when blood and night air coat them
and she was sleeping
until they beat her into a darkness
that holds neither sleep nor dreams
and I remember being afraid
of the cold, of the dark, of the unknown,
when I slept on concrete
so many years ago
not yet understanding
who I truly needed to fear
because she was sleeping
and when she finally died
surrounded by hospital whites
she couldn't see
and beeping, breathing machines
she couldn't hear
I wonder if her nightmares
went searching
not for the two
who would never be true men
those two angry killers
but for their two friends
who stood there
and watched her die
little by little
as each kick and fist
satisfied some lack of responsibility
some lack of humanity
too many of us share

"Put it on my tab."

Carla Kandinsky

"Wine 'em and dine 'em my boss
said. Put it on my tab. Sleep in
tomorrow." My evening was
spent in the company of three
gentlemen from abroad, who
didn't snap pictures, get drunk,
or ask for girls. No, we were
all quite serious, closing the deal
as if our very lives depended on it.

Next morning I woke with
a roar in my head, the gates of
hell bursting open, the Twin
Towers where I worked were
splitting, burning, crashing. I
watched from my window,
knowing on any other day I
would have been there.

Somebody saved me, God,
three dark men in suits, the
luck of the draw that I took
them to dinner, the evening
that earned me this morning's
business deal that
my life depended on.

Gone

BOB CLIFFORD

George told me my old rat-
trap house burned down
along with the ground
fair amount of looking up to adult world was
spent in between the
leaves and grass
until we would roll off
the stone wall and end on our
heads figuring how come
god did not like nice catholic
boys with food stamp
supplies
to squirm down your
throat
a dead rat in the bathroom
people downstairs with a
broken piano
top bunk bed provided the
longest sleep from noise
the eyesore of one street and town is gone

Volcano Watch

Alex Miloradovich

Vesuvius is quiet tonight.
The land partied out,
out of rhyme,
smoked like cigarettes
time and time again.

Placid night
ingenuously dull,
flaccid, altogether calm.

No storm is brewing here.
The atmosphere instead imbued,
with armies of demographic acronyms
scheming bed-wise,
venal delusions
greedy for oblivious sleep.

And the innocent immortalized,
plaster cast,
dreaming otherwise
in pumice-clad agonies.

In This Deceptive Weather
for Valerie

ROBERT LAVETT SMITH

In this deceptive weather, time expands
Like the salt-sodden moisture in the air
That finds a foothold nearly everywhere:
Long hours fall to nothing in our hands.
Anyone who has loved you understands
Breathless exhilaration, dull despair,
A passion none would hesitate to declare
Lasting and real, exacting no demands.
This atmosphere erases what we were
Offers no hint of what we may become
Your beauty is immediate—is *here*—
But makes the yearning days the more lonesome.
In the moist darkness of your eyes, are there
No promises of anywhere like home?

12/24/94

Nancy Wilson

Today
50 people
were killed
in Sri Lanka
by a gunman
& I mourn
my cat
Today
the tears wash over me
as I ride
the bus
from Alameda
to Berkeley
to work
with strangers
floating by
& I mourn
for
My lost
Cat.
And President
Clinton
participating in
peace talks
in the
Middle East—
Israel & Jordan
and 22

or was
it 21
Jews
killed
right before
this historic
event
by the PLO
And my
Cat of
fourteen
years
my wonderful black
& white
large cat
RALPH
is gone.
The World looks
Bleak.

Tenderloin novice yearns for Dolores Park …

David Sher

Tenderloin novice yearns for Dolores Park.
Not Beau Dekker.
Walks in the gutter to sidestep bad block on Turk.
Eats at Tony's & Ride only when on empty.
Runs to Golden Gate's GAAP when welfare is threatened.
Seeks solace and storage with the Fools on Hyde.
Sees those who work to fix what's broken.

Hope and desperation side by side,
Warehoused in boxes of ticky tacky.
Fear driven greed has stolen the market.
We all turn into caricatures of ourselves
When our sun goes down.

Chapter 3

Oh, the Millionaire/Billionaire CEOs

Mary Rudge

Oh, the CEOs, the CEOs,
they all know where the profit goes,
and they go away with the money to play
and you won't see them here.
Oh the CEOs, the CEOs
they never shop with Mom and Pop,
or stand by you at the Taco Truck
with your thrift-store cup
on your coffee break,
or in take-out lines
at the noodle shop
as you count out your change—
and rush home from work
so you can feed your family.

Oh the CEOs, the CEOs,
they never pay tax on their
hidden dough
And maybe we know where
the greedy go
and we'll never follow them
down below
but share what we've got
and somehow care for
the other poor—
—let's make each other happy here.

Go Back Where You Came From

Daniel Marlin

(In March 2012 Shaima Alwadi of El Cajon, California, received an anonymous note which read, "Go back to your own country..." A week later she was found murdered on her living room floor.)

    Let's say you took your own advice,
    and went back
    where you came from,
    to the tubercular slums of Glasgow
    a hundred and fifty years ago,

    or the peat farms of starving Galway.

    Or to Moledetchna,
    where Jewish boys
    changed their names to dodge
    twenty year hitches
    in the Czar's infantry,

    or to Reggio Calabria
    when landowners
    had their way with peasant girls,
    as they worked their parents
    into dry furrows.

    Try going back, not as a tourist
    with credit card, but clueless,
    in the humble shawls
    your forebears wore
    gathering lice in steerage,

before they poured off the docks,
to have the long syllables of their names
lopped off by an Immigration officer
checking for signs of palsy,
scanning his list of anarchists.

Sail backward,
past ports of departure,
through centuries as soldiers
hiding your religion
or killing for it,
as wet nurses,
unable to feed your own.

Back through the winters of the Rhineland,
Bohemia, Piemonte,
along trails of forgotten migration,
down the millennial ladder
to ancient African valleys
where your great mothers
learned to walk upright.

—But don't stop there.
Forage with pointed snout
for grubs among ferns,
beneath the shadows of pterodactyls,

re-enter the primal ocean,
before our fins became toes,
and our lungs began
their subtle duty.

Become again
the one-celled flares of life

we were,

and continue—

into elemental stardust,
the whirlwind of the black
invisible hand.

Untitled

FORREST CURO

My Heart is sick of being right.
Liars, fellow-cowards, fools caught
between God and Satan, listen!
Isn't it time for
honest yearning?
Haven't we had enough
of being too wise to trust?

I can take disappointment; I cannot
endure another year's prudence.
Roll back the sky, shatter
my face with a terror of angels
but make me yours, God!

Another stillborn Christmas
and another, and another?
Wake us! I've seen enough
of reasonable expectations.
Let me babble incoherent
prophecies of mercy coming, mercy here!
with only our need as evidence

and may the dead rise singing hallelujah
before I worry anymore
what people think!

The Luxury of Well-Made Furniture

Dale Jensen

    on seventy-third avenue
    i saw a kid
    who looked about ten
    with a cellphone
    in a dealer's pose
    leaning against a telephone pole

    two times on the bus
    different men behind me
    talking about parole

    my front door is shut
    my drinking glass is half full of water
    and has been like that for hours
        if i leave it like that for months   for years
        there will be dust accumulated all over it
        will the dust gather?   will it precipitate?
    when the bus passes all the horror
    of the way poor people have to live in this country
    i understand but i don't understand how it must feel
        the dust from my middle class upbringing
        the numbness in her voice as she calls emergency
        as the old man lies gasping on his foreign rug
        and the luxury of well-made furniture
        becomes dimmer   dimmer
        to his eyes

    and the bus passes the chalk outline
    of a human body on the sidewalk
    and a block later you can't see it anymore

Un Invierno en Nueva York (Tamborsuenyo Remix)

BERNARDO GONZALES

    El senyor "Don" Quixote presente
      en mente
        conversaciones en oraciones
        desde
          la mosca del Senyor Presidente
          quemado de fe
        casi tostado
        hablando con todos tipos de testigos de Jehova
       perdidos a veces en sus missiones sagrados
      llevando aquas bendidas por los pueblos y
     los pueblos de pajaros mas conejos y buffalos
    todos bautizados por los fuegos de ricos

    Y quien sabe
      finalemente
        si importa o no
          pero a veces veo santos
          caminando sin zapatos
         en la nieve sucia de invierno
        santos perdidos con un regalo navidenyo
       y sus ojos pegados al cielo
       como Coltrane el tecato
      y un olor duro como punyos
      tocando tambores puede ser
     como el ninyo que toco por Jesucristo
    un regalito de Tumbao
    y quien sabe que vale
     cada loco con su momento

cada momento de la vida
　de cada Jesucristo
　　de cada Maria de la Vaca-sin-Pesetas-Sanchez-Mira
　　veo santos y les doy comida, conversacion, cuarto,
　　　y fe
　　　　en el sentido
　　　　que Dios te ha dado
　　　　 un regalo por el mundo
　　　　asi es como creo
　　　　y mi regalo es asi

A Winter in New York (Dreamdrum Remix)

Bernardo Gonzales

    El senyor Don Quixote present
      of mind
        conversations in prayers
       from since
         the fly in El Senyor Presidente
          burnt by faith
        almost toasted
       talking with all kinds of witnesses of Jehovah
      lost sometimes in their sacred missions
     carrying blessed water for the pueblos and
    the pueblos of birds plus rabbits and buffaloes
   all of them baptized by the fires of ricos

And who knows
    finally
      if it matters or not
        but at times I see saints
      walking without shoes
        in the dirty snow of winter
        saints lost with a christmas present
       and their eyes glued to the sky
      like Coltrane the addict
      and an odor hard as uppercuts
     playing congas maybe
   like the little boy who played for Baby Jesus
a little gift of Tumbao
 and who knows what's important
   each nut with their own moment

of each Jesus Christ
   of each Maria de la Vaca-sin-Pesetas-Sanchez-Mira
    I see saints and give them food, conversation, room,
    and faith
     in the sense
      that God has given you
     a gift for the world
    that's how I believe
  and my gift is like that

Idolatic Power

Rennon

THAT WELL IS NOT THREATENING!!!
It is too remote, too ancient, almost forgotten!
Wells are not subversive, violent, or inclined towards
terrorism!
What, pray tell, are you talking about?

FALL IN!!!
See how instantly that well will
Redefine, threatening for you!

Well walls too high to scale?
Mud, with an everlasting lust for flesh
HYPOTHERMIC NIGHT!!

Why did you approach?

Need for water?
Curious about your reflection;
after being seduced by your own vanity?
You like playing footsies with your suicidal side?
WHAT WILL YOU DO NOW?
Scream out? Pray a little,
Let that mud have its morsel of meat?

WHAT IS YOUR IDOLATRIC DU-JOUR
What god did you worship this morning?
A reflection of the sun in the mirror?

DID YOU TASTE IDOLATRIC MILK FROM
Your auto? That dollar bill in your pocket?
Perhaps a person, place or thing
You call home?
The GOVERNMENT, NASA,
Your foot patrolman, a priest?
The brilliance, dazzle, potency of the sun itself?
IDOLATRIC POWER

Good night sweet prince.

They Are the Ones

Keith Savage

When you keep a people ignorant
    you can teach them whatever you want
They will accept the word as reason
    it's really no special stunt
When people are trained against God
    there is confusion under <u>this</u> sun
Just as man created a monster
    the same fosters, rebellion
The secret societies of this world
    plot against Abraham's seed
<u>S</u>ocieties <u>A</u>dvancing <u>T</u>oward <u>A</u>nti-Christ <u>N</u>ation
    keep the people in need
The CIA, a covert group
    teach others to rape with rats
While the president—the son of the head
    says "Hey—look at that!"
To use God's name to speak <u>falsely</u>
    while they fill the world with lies
A prayer from the <u>people</u> is needed
    our redemption, it draws me
Religion, too broad a word
    it may hide a grim disguise
The persons concerned with God's purpose
    they are the ones to try
    they are the ones to fly.

LONELINESS

Rashna

SILENTLY, LONELINESS EATS AWAY AT YOUR EMOTIONS.
TRYING TO ENDURE AND SEEK COMFORT AND EASE.
YET, SILENTLY, LONELINESS IS EATING AWAY AT YOUR HEART.
YOUR SOUL SEEKING COMFORT AND EASE.
FALSE CONVERSATION WITH NO MEANING AS WE LIE QUIETLY.
NOT A WORD BETWEEN US.
THE SPACE IS GETTING LARGER AND THE HOPES OF CLOSING BECOME SLIMMER EACH DAY.
UNAWARE OF THE SILENT KILLER, LONELINESS.
LONELINESS IS NO LONGER A STATE OF MIND, BUT A STATE OF BEING.
LONELINESS TO BE TOLD HOW WONDERFUL YOU ARE STILL WAITING.
HOW LIFE WOULD BE UNTHINKABLE WITHOUT YOUR BODY NEAR.
LONELINESS IS NO WORD.
A STATE OF MIND THAT IS REAL AND COLD.
ALONE WITH SOMEONE WHO REFUSES TO ACKNOWLEDGE YOU IN PUBLIC.
LONELINESS THEN BECOMES ALL ALONE.
NOW IT'S REAL!
LONELINESS COULD NOT JUST BE YOU BUT ME ALSO.
ALONE WITH LONELINESS.

Three Days Retreat

Susan Knutson

    I descended into the belly of homelessness
       Three days and nights I lived inside this belly looking out
         Standing waiting for food
          Standing waiting for shelter
           WALKING_WALKING_WALKING
DIRTY HAIR AND BODY
    STINKING AND DIRTY CLOTHES
       WATCHING THE STRONG DESIRE TO SURVIVE

I WRITE TO EXPLAIN TO MYSELF

The Brut or *Le Difference*

JOHN RHODES

Strange hint; the smell of a tenderloin: Brutal, with the power to make you mute.

Preferably the hint would be better known as a manly clue, rather than something like the hint of pneumonia or the flu.

These hints can be awful and a hint of the end, where things are unlawful and make the mind bend.

No love is remembered from this shallow smell; the one that "seemed" to bother no one, but nobody would tell.

No token of balance of men and women exists ... because of this Tender-loin men will shake their fists.

Clean face, clean clothes, are reminders to men who know this hint, so brutal to the nose; not the smell of a bum, but someone more brutal and not homespun; lock him up in your mind, where there are thoughts that bind.

Barely Divorced

Gail Ford

Now
every time I try to write
I fall asleep

Eyelids droop then drop
Warm anchors
that all my will can
barely get to
flutter.

Flicker.
A thin line
of light
then darkness.

The pen wobbles
in my gone-liquid
hand.

Let me just sleep.

Engage only in dreams,
in the soft fog cloud buffer
of far away-ing if not actually
leaving.

Let me just be afloat
on a cool green sea
that laps against
each inch by inch of me.

Drifting where no two
thoughts need fit together.
Where there is nothing
to understand. Untangle.

Nothing to unwind.

Except perhaps this binding sheet.
This so, so thin cloth
that straps one ankle to its next.
That wraps my arms
to my chest.
That binds even my chin
and cheeks.

This papyrus-like cloth
that rustles between my naked skin
and the rough wood
of this woman-sized coffin
I didn't even know
I was in.

Morning Falls

Bill Mercer

Morning falls through my window
Like a wounded soldier

Outside on my doorstep
A folded newspaper bleeds.
It bleeds on all our doorsteps
All across this land.
There is blood on my hands
When I pick it up,
There is blood on all our hands.

The muffled screams
Of the tortured
Are folded away inside.
The shattered dreams
Of the innocent
Find no place to hide.
The smoking wreck
That was Fallujah,
The stench of all that died.
The broken neck
Of Baghdad.
The bodies stack up inside.

The blood on all our hands
Is folded away inside.

For Amadou Diallo, Killed by the NYPD

Julia Vinograd

In a dark place
where he didn't have a gun
he reached for a wallet he carried.
The cops shot him in self defense
and he'll never be 23.
There's a framed picture of him
teaching his son to walk,
the child grasps one finger in each hand
and they're both laughing.
The picture's on top of a small bookcase
in a house that will never be built
and the child will never be born.
How many people did the cops kill
in self defense
when they thought he was someone else?
So many bullets. The 19 that hit him
for all the children and grandchildren
he'll never have, and the rest of the 41
for all his children's lovers,
wives, husbands, friends.
So many people in one man's skin
and each got a bullet with their name on it
and the only name the cops had was wrong.
They had the name of a killer with a gun
in a dark place
and they shot in self defense.
But his name was in his wallet with his ID.
He tried to show them and he died
in a dark place.
Too dark, too long.

Dedication Speech for the George W. Bush Sewage Plant

Alfred Turi

It's not every day that our country
enjoys a president as special as you.
George, you've been a great role model
of all the possibilities of the American Dream.

An America where failure don't mean a thing
where the pesky truth don't stop us
from declaring mission accomplished
where no child left behind means
even a C student can grow up to be president. For two terms!

George, we're gonna miss you when these eight years are up
Who will remind us that it's ok to take two months off every year
to clear some brush on the family farm?
Who will remind us that it's ok to be blissfully ignorant
of all them foreign troubles in the world?

George, your missions accomplished are many.
You've given a generation of soldiers
the privilege of dying for their country.
You've outdone the environmentalists
and let the market curb our addiction to oil.

There's one thing you haven't done, though,
and that is you've never set foot in San Francisco
but no worries. For today we are here honored
to set our foot down on you.

Teardrop
for Rico Hill

Michelle Bindhill

    TATTOOED UNDER CORNER OF
                  YOUR EYE
FROZEN BLUE LIKE THE BARREL
               OF YOUR GUN
CUZ WE BOTH KNOW
    YOU'D NEVER LET IT GO
ALWAYS MOVING ALWAYS RUNNING
    AS FAST AS YOU CAN
THE MAN THE BEEF
    YOU NEVER OUTRAN
LYING ON YOUR RACK
TRYING NOT TO CARE
KNOWING IN YOUR HEART
IT'S NEVER EVER FAIR
THE THINGS THEY DO
THE THINGS THEY SAY
JUST LIKE STEEL BARS
THESE WALLS OF GRAY
WILL NEVER CHANGE
    REARRANGE
OR GO AWAY
FROZE FOREVER
CONCRETE SOLID LIKE THE WALLS OF THEIR SUN
THE BLUE TATTOO   TEARDROP
    ENGRAVED ON YOUR SKIN

be it ever so humble

Atlantis

Trap spiders live
Beneath the ground.
Birds build nests of clay and straw.
Penguins lay their eggs on snow,
All blackbirds nest and caw.
Polar bears, in arctic terrain,
Protect their cubs
From sleet and rain,
Rats live in sewers
The world around,
And on millionaire's yachts,
Wherever they're found.
Esquimieux live in igloos,

The Bantu lives in the bush.
Even the lonely albatross
Has a place to put his tush.
Squirrels build nests high in a tree,
And, sometimes, in the ground.
Butterflies build on the back of leaves,
At least, the ones I've found.
Mermaids keep their tails under water,
Along with fish and whales.
Bats live in caves,
Vampires, in graves,
And criminals live in jail.
Cars live in parking garages,

Clothes, in laundromats.
Dogs have their very own houses,

And there's a special house just for cats.
Some birds live in cages,
Gold-plated, but a cage, just the same.
There's a place to rest, or some kind of nest
For just about everything you can name.
Things and people sleep all over the world,
In everything you can see.
How come, no matter what I do,
You can't find room for ME?

Plug

Clyde Gallagher

Sing a Sesame Street sunrise strumming guitar Kindergarten gardens, eyeballs swirling O's drenched in Alphabet wet soup. Raposo rapped kaleidoscope singalongs in all the colors of the rainbow, brown, mauve, purple Muppet people smiling ABCs of sticky, lovely, drooling change. Roosevelt Franklin is a Ying Yaged prophet, like Beethoven's funk Bass, or Parliament Funkadelic's brass stringed Wings.

String songs simple, string songs strong, string song LOUD to last your whole life long. Raposo gave as Generations got, and the Best Minds of my Time didn't worry if they were good enough in a speck of spot of TV brought to you today by the letter E.

But that Peanut Butter Piper went on Up, as John John grew up and Grunge grew out loud, expanding songs' lungs, nailing Sesame Street to Screaming Trees. 1991 clashed piano's Don Music in Doctor Martin's leather, though somewhere in the Weather, Joe Raposo dances Pearl Jam's singalongs, tumbling cookie crumb boulders down Nirvana's checkered flannel, laughing happy and proud in silly white clown clouds.

So give now, please, give up your alms, so that Big yellow Bird may still have a home. Let Snuffleupagus yet exist existentially six, trunk swinging long, leading the world in a belly full of song. Please plug into Public Broadcasting with your tax-free donation.

Is it for Freedom

Sara Thompsen

Rulers of the nations as you fuss and fight
Over who owns the soil and who has the right
To design, build, to sell and store and fire
All the bombs and guns to defend your holy empire

There are children hungry, children sick and dying
There are mothers, fathers, sisters, brothers crying
They're only pawns in your play of power and corruption
Slowly starved in your new weapon of mass destruction

And prove to me America that you care
And prove to me America, you're aware
Who's dying for your freedom is this land
Who pays the cost for the liberties you demand

Is it for freedom or a comfort and convenience
Is it to profit for big business, we pledge our allegiance
Are we prisoners in the land of the brave and the bold
Held by indifference or hearts grown hard and cold

And prove to me America, that you care
And prove to me America, that you're aware
Who's dying for your freedom is this land
Who pays the cost for the liberties you demand

Chapter 4

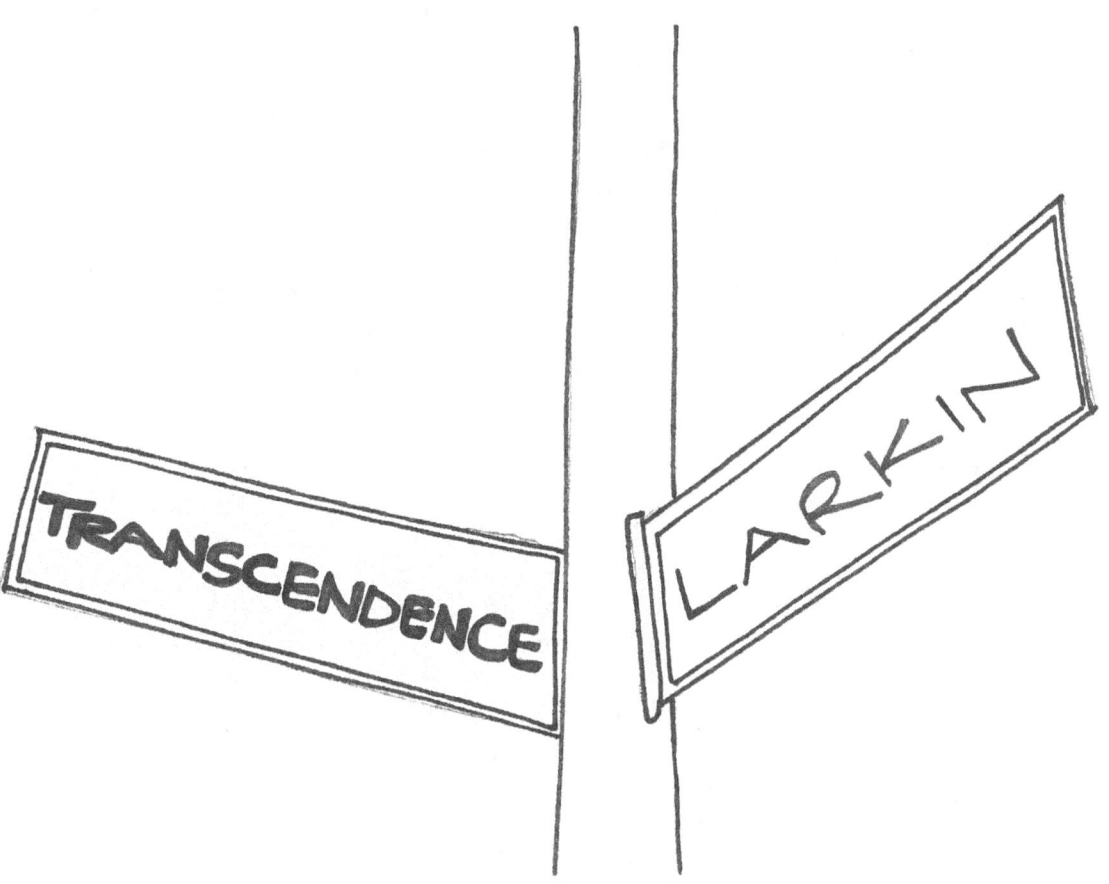

Living in the Land of the Dead

T. Hayes

From sun up to sun down in every city and all towns, there is a lurk of the unknown that keeps us on the edge of our stoops or benches or blocks or your ergonomic chairs. Timid individuals turn to the unknown for relief or simply to steer clear away from the mute sound of a congregation pleading their sorrows. The unknown can be anywhere at any time so during any weekend day folk run to beer and wine. For others it's just a normal occurrence so when it comes it's boiling water off the back. No one is immune from this cycle; it's mighty as well as arrogant and large as a brontosaurus. There's no particular state, city, or race that has it worse because it's viral but yet attractive. Although it's ugly and sometimes senseless; we are forced to deal with it, with tight hearts to make a bright moon shine through San Francisco's fog.

    Every change isn't great especially when one changes for the worst. It takes more for this to succeed. It takes more, but enough of what it is. Sirens, police brutality, racism, lack of opportunities, poor education, good organization, terrible staff, sameness. This is the unknown being known for its true name... Dead! Enough of this can have a person going to St. Anthony's for mental health counseling. Enough can get a person to commit the ultimate meaning heading to the golden gate bridge and leaping to the unknown. No longer living life among what's dead. You have to be here to know it, and understand what needs to be done for a change that's significant but inspiring. Change lanes of self-destruction change planning that's designed by the dead.

    The dead don't sleep; it dances from tune to tune staying far away from jazz. Its mind is made and it chooses to dance around jazz. If I told you, "You are pretty" would you believe me? If I told you, "You are smart" would you believe me? When I say, "Living among the dead without doing a damn thing about it" you better believe we are fucked.

They say, "Wait a while longer housing is coming." I say. "Really." They say, "Trust us, we know what were doing." I say, "That's what those unarmed men was doing when they were shot by cops." They replied, "That's not true we're just not the same." I say, "I know 'cause sameness comes with a price."

We pay with green money: Sometimes with red blood. We wear clothes the same. What deadness is you to tell me we ain't? We are not identical, but if you got the right to marry anyone; why can't he? or why can't she? She can be a he or vice versa. This is the city. We share it the same. You can say "same" and I can say likewise there we saying the same damn thang. My skin is smooth and dark; yours may be light and smooth. We go to the beach we gone be fighting for the s.p.f. Being haunted by racist standardization is dead. It kills the root of the so-called American dream.

The dream of opportunity has never been in the hands of many. I'm one of the bunch. Having to fight is something that comes out of the unknown. The unknown used to like to stay anonymous. But now each day it's becoming easier to see. In all these colors that the dead don't like. The message has to be "I'm living in the land to wake the dead," out of depression, out of substance abuse and into conscience thinking to remind them of the opportunity they have to change the circumstances around them. Hurry! To the meeting—there's a sliver of bright moon shining through this foggy Frisco weather.

Emergency Room Flashback

Judy Wells

41st and Telegraph
Firemen/paramedics
in black gear
with green fluorescent stripes
and helmets
ready for combat
surround a thin black man
with plastic tubes up his nose
sitting against a wall
staring blankly into space
helpless, hopeless.

The well-fed firemen joke,
do busy paramedic things,
while a small brown boy
sits patiently
beside the thin black man
who can do no fathering.

We hurry by
to the Asmara Restaurant
where beautiful Eritreans
will serve us food.
I glance back
at the thin black man
without claim to his body
helpless, hopeless
and inside I cry:
I have been there,
my brother.

Hayward April

Marek Breiger

Portuguese Square. Homeless men, some sleeping on the benches, others drinking wine, standing on the tiles that form a map of the Azore Islands. Traffic streams by. Sixty years ago there were small farms here and immigrants worked and lived in this place. It was a slower time of streetcars and trains and open views of the Bay.

And more than fifty years ago Japanese Americans were herded here, forced from their homes as if they were alien strangers instead of neighbors and friends.

And the men drinking wine have their own community, one a stranger can sympathize with or condescend to, but cannot easily understand or enter.

And still on the streets—whether you drive or walk—you can see acts of kindness and acts too of cruelty.
Under an April sky, so soft and blue.

Lost to all the world

MOCONNOR

I went for a walk today, hunched in my fading parka against the cold, wet air. Grey November, 6 days now since defeat, since the world view I savor was bested, fairly or not. How would a "red" American feel this path, I wondered? How would these stones feel beneath her feet? Would the hawk's cry sound differently? Would her steps be more hopeful? Certain? Mandated? The path taken *this way!* Fallujah taken *this way!* Darfur avoid *this way!* And the homeless folk huddled around the picnic grill, warming up together beside the leaping flames of old newspapers. Vets among them. The Native American Vet I see on occasion, smiling always when greeted. Vietnam a mere thought away, just a step away upon these stones whose press yet sends a Red American, healing. Yes, this muted cluster, in familiar camouflage, how would a "red" American meet their grizzled gaze? With compassionate conservatism? And how, how would we, walking in opposite directions, meet each other's eyes? (With a quiet smile, perhaps; nod of the head, our true knowing of each other only a question away?) How, how can we both see this same world rent with such cruel divide and not wonder: *"Am I wrong?"*

And might we, in that wondering, embrace the World's whole family again?

I'm out of poems (for now). Estrangement doesn't lend itself to melody, at least not to melody that I can bear.

War on terror? Peace on Earth?
Oh Beloved of Bethlehem,
(less than a stone's throw away),
how, how do we all rejoin the pilgrimage
into forgiveness?

Remember Surrounded

David T. Murphy

Still near the Lodi Bridge
there is a copse of cedars,
box elders, and cottonwoods
—all that's left of a wind break.

Listen: there were meadowlarks,
thrushes, red-winged blackbirds,
nuthatches, robins
and one spring noon
the remaining ice fell like crystal from the trees
onto the thawing surface of the slender,
twisted vein of the River Vermilion.

We were surrounded by that
and the scent of loam.
Your gaze became mine.
I can still feel our breathing.

In the cities were the soft shouts
of thou shalt not and the voices
of other vows
    many voices distinctly shouting
        thou shalt not

Still there in South Dakota,
flatter and vaster than this page,
despite the voices that called us
and the decades since,
I am glad that near the Lodi Bridge
we gave ourselves that noon.

I Have Become My True Self

Amun (via Metu)

I have become my True Self.
I watched my old self die with my Spirit's eye.
My old self said to me,
"You will die if you kill me,
You will not be able to see this world anymore."
I continued watching from a distance and yet very near, at
how my old self was being slaughtered by me, within me.
"Die!" I said, "Die!"
"You are nothing but an illusion that hides my True Self.
You are just a costume soon to be recycled on earth.
I will not listen to you anymore!"
"I will not die, I will live forever"
My old self insisted,
"What about your family, friends, husband …
Will you leave them behind?
They need you and you need them!"
"No! They will not leave me, and
I will not leave them.
We are all one,
One in existence, one in purpose.
I am in them and they are in me.
We will soon meet each other and become one.
You will no longer control me with this
illusion of division anymore!"
"Die!" I said, "Die!"
My old self was defeated
and shortly after left my mind!
I entered another stage of mind,

I felt a great feeling of joy and happiness
All that I remember, is just "being!"
I was myself, I became myself, and I was myself again.
I became my True Self!

What I Am Learning

JOSHUA MANN

I don't know who I am,
but slowly I'm learning who I am not.
I am not the guilt and shame I sometimes feel,
nor am I the trauma and the pain,
nor the fear or the sorrow.
And slowly
ever so slowly
I'm learning to accept
what I didn't expect
and greet it with my eyes and arms open.

Voices

MIKE NIEMCZYK

And he heard a poet
and tried to imitate
that particular voice
heard through
the confessional window,
and she heard a poet
and got down on her knees
praying and praising,
and yet another heard a poet
and walked through the woods,
the rain barely ended,
and they kept writing and writing,
sometimes hearing
entirely different voices than before,
and they wrote 'til they fell over
and then got up and wrote again,
and sometimes
in the dead of night
or at the earliest crack of morning
you'd swear all their voices
sang together
or perhaps just created
a glorious cacophony,
the main thing is
they kept on writing,
throughout it all
they kept on singing.

Whiff

Jeffery Marlin

If anything, Joan is
Less patient than I am
With monotheistic impediments
To acceptable thought and action.

Keep the tunes and triptychs, we say,
But stow the endless beseeching.
We do not allude to the Buddha.
Nor do we leave it to Shiva.

I sit in our kitchen alcove.
She stands in front of the sink
Explaining a practice she advocates
With her neonatal nurses;

Each expiring newborn
Is held in the moment it passes;
None will go alone.

Twenty years later
I cannot remember
Without a surge in my throat

And the whiff
Of religion born in
A nighttime fire.

Why do I sit long …

YOLANDA WRIGHT

Why do I sit long
to flow out a rhythm of
verse
knowing—
if I just pick up a pencil
I may be heard

Thoughts that recycle—
the mind, reads to flourish—
even before a time

Who says words of thought take
space
they are of time, space— and thought
conveyed
    sort of a translation
     so I write my thoughts
   as they come to me
    or—
maybe, I see how they sound
to ME.

I Saw a Man Today

Mary Nordkwelle

I saw a man today
Who runs his own business
His life is dedicated
And he works night and day

He took time out of his
Busy schedule
To see me.
To take me to lunch
But we never ate
We walked around Berkeley
Seeing the sights,
The campus, museum
And Telegraph Road.

Then I caught the BART
Back into town
And someone asked me
If I'd assassinate Bush
I said why ask me?
It is because I was in
San Quentin this morning
  Visiting a friend?

On the streets of San Francisco
I saw many homeless people

—One was dancing

And I thought
Who is really free?
The man who works day and night
   For his company
The man on Death Row
   In his tiny cell—
Or the person on the street?

Untitled

Dee Allen

These streets are watching
You with many eyes.

These streets are watching
You from lightposts above intersections
Of traffic, in the "worst" parts of any
Given metropolis.
Squadcars turn each corner,
Anticipating someone's false move,
A potential arrest.

These streets are secure now
With many electric eyes and extra cops.
The repressive flavor is almost
Commonplace enough to be ecology.

Everyone is a suspect.
Criminals in the making.

Is the crime gone?
Are the drugs gone?
Are the gangs locked away?
Are we safer yet?

These streets are probing
Your intimate moments.
That couple kissing in the plaza has a
Closed-circuit captive audience.

The all-seeing eye of the state
Can watch your move, wherever you go, at any
Given moment.
But its main gatekeeper
Has a massive pile of skeletal matter
In his closet.
A closet that just overflowed,
Bones and all—

Come to the land of the Golden Gate
Where sanctuary and protection can be provided
To souls   fleeing poverty which has no boundaries,
Corporate reign
Over their plane
Of existence

    And to racist reactionaries
Who want them removed
Before it becomes
"A Third World Slum of the North."

Blindness

Ralph Dranow

The big black woman
Lined, leathery face,
Unsmiling eyes,
Is selling Street Spirit
Outside Whole Foods.
"I already have one,"
I tell her.
"Smoke is coming from your car,"
She says,
Pointing to the hood.
"I don't see any smoke."
She gives me a stern look,
Repeats insistently,
"Smoke is coming from your car."
I don't see it,"
I respond curtly,
Thinking she must be crazy.
Maybe she's angry
I didn't buy Street Spirit.
Her eyes flicker over my face
Like a puzzled camera.

Returning from a short trip
The next day
I notice wisps of smoke
Billowing from the hood.
Remorse whispers in my ear:
You're so quick to judge
And she was just trying to help you.

together ... alone ... awake

Matt Wolf

revel in the beauty of dreams
with the lithe dove in the pasture
view the azure landscape imbued with jasmine
walk home past the willows
feel the light gale embrace the skin

reflect on pale yellow roses
retreat past the worn, red barn door
the hinges creak faintly
wind rushes gently
grey clouds fill in the sky once again

another bright day has passed into eve
grey clouds fill the sky once again
they wait until night when they know
we'll be lying in bed listening
to the clock ticking slow

The Philosophical Forest

GARY BOLSTRIDGE

If a tree fell in an Existential forest
would anyone hear it?
Would the tree exist unless someone saw it?
And if they saw it, wouldn't they hear it?

If a tree fell in a Metaphysical forest
 would I fall with it and blame God?

If a tree fell in a Surreal forest
would it turn into a table with bare feet
walking across hot sand
full of holes with tiger paws swiping
at a leg made of dripping cheese?

If a tree fell in a Pataphysical forest
would it land upside down on its hands
and become a chair
containing the Seat of Knowledge
without knowing anything?

If a tree fell in a Buddhist forest
would it close its eyes
and meditate on just being wood
and lose its leaves and flowers
and branches and roots
and just be a tree?

If a tree fell in an Idealist forest
and we heard it
would it really have fallen
if we didn't think about it?
And would we even need trees in a perfect
    forest?

If a tree fell in a Transcendental forest
would the tree know it?
If a tree fell in a Catholic forest
would it continuously berate itself
and repeat *It's all my fault*?

If a tree fell in a Newtonian forest
would it hit you on the head
and then fall to the ground?

If a tree fell in a Nietzschean forest
would each tree have repeated
the same event over time?

If a tree fell in a Pragmatic forest
would it have happened
until we cut the tree into toothpicks?

If a tree fell in a National Forest
would the company be fined for illegal logging
trespassing, destroying a National Treasure
and the habitat of some tit-bird or mouse?
Or would they just be stimulating the economy?

If a tree fell in a Rational forest
would it just die?

Poetry

Alexandra Loonin

poetry is not an exclusive beauty, it's an angle
a way of seeing feeling appreciating communication
expressions

we're channeling each other on these frequencies not because
we're special
but because we can
and it's a forceful liberation to speak the soul
to caress the source of self by explaining to someone else
what they already know
to listen to your own story through the hands of others
to be and be forgiven by never being condemned and
believing in a light you've never seen
substance untouchable for the solid skin mind relief
thoughts born before the thought's existence,
perceived as imagination
tracing knowledge
back and back again

you don't know me looking at my face
you know me by knowing yourself
and then will we be strong enough to lose ourselves
to find each other
realizing they're both the same
so see me, not a poetic expression
see you, not the ways of your words

see us, the beginning and end of a composition written on
ancient timetables
where poetry is not an exclusive beauty
but a contact ad sent to the Fair Lady in utter desperation
hoping for response, answered while written, ending in a p.s.
life alone
is beauty.

Out There

Owen Dunkle

The lonely L Car   of Jack Spicer
On top of the world.
It is much like body
Surfing down, down to
The beach and the roaring
Tides that tithe. Great
Abandon, the coastline
Thin and stretches for miles.
Love and the great eternity
Mocking the small waves.

The salt smell,
The grail of clouds.
Runners, dogs, and campfires.
Kelp, bare feet, the seagulls
Reach the night.

The flight of sparrows,
Bicyclists, atheists, and altruists,
Silentious abandon of the SF
Evening.

The Visitor

Martha Boesing

I stand in the open doorway of my house.
I am an old woman
and I know nothing.
My house is made of clay.
There are no curtains on the windows;
the wind has blown them down
long, long ago.
The wooden floors are bare,
but they are clean enough.
You come into my house.
You bring flowers for the table.
They bloom even after you are gone.
We share the evening meal.
You are a guest in my house.
You are welcome here forever,
for there are no secrets between us.
I want to tell you this:
I stand all day in the doorway of this house.
I stand leaning against the portal,
Enjoying the morning sun.
A fly buzzes round the frame.
I hold a bowl in my hands.
It is made of clay and like my house,
and it is empty.
I don't know what to put in it;
I know nothing.
I stand in the doorway of this house
enjoying the morning sun.

I do this every day.

And I want to tell you this:
as you come in and you go out,
She, too, comes in: She, too, goes out,
a guest like you, in my house —
She the Unnamable One,
the One who will not let me go.
She sits at the table with us,
in the silence,
before we share our meal.
I want to tell you this:
Sometimes She is a bird;
her wings beat against my heart.
Sometimes She is a river,
a white flame;
She races through my blood
And sometimes
She lifts me in her arms
and She shows me
everything;
towns, cities, trees, mountains,
people —
desperate
to do well.
I see everything.
Everything,
bursting to be born!
I want to tell you this
for there are not secrets between us.
I want to tell you this,
even though you know as well as I,
even though there are no words to tell it,
and I know nothing.

I want to tell you this:
Sometimes, I am not tired;
Sometimes, for a moment,
I am awake.

To tell you this is to say: I am your friend
It is to say: I see you dancing
It is to say: hello.
I love you.

Life Among the Gemini

Jesse James Johnson

I live among the Gemini/ twins who sleep/ in a twist of limbs/ speak in riddles/ and love/ in knots of hallucinations/ I hear many voices/ water nymphs in the toilet bowl/ conjured friends/ psychiatrists/ hallways whispering the wrong directions/ holy apparitions weeping.

I go walking/ seeking solace in/ the noise of traffic/ and still they call/ from the canyon's walls of a thousand windows/ from every rooftop/ in the Tenderloin/ I am sick of them/ I hate their voices/ the idiots and oracles/ that fill my ears/ with prophecies, lamentations and mindless gossip.

They pull my clothing/ urging me to follow/ as they descend into the gutter's throat/ where a mind can be lost and not recover/ from the darkness of the underground tunnels/ I pull away/ stick to the sidewalk/ I concentrate on neon signs / and traffic lights/ refusing the seductive whispers/ of Hades and valium.

Exhausted/ I light a cigarette/ exhale/ and sit myself on the/ concrete steps/ of an entryway/ guarded by Chinese dogs/ soon enough/ a woman steps up around me/ rattling the gate that bars her way/ screaming/ let me in/ the sky is heavy/ I need my pills.

The response is a glassy silence/ she rattles harder/ strong as an orangutan/ I'm impressed/ but the well-lit hallway remains impassive/ I offer her a cigarette/ no/ thanks she says/ not my poison/ I can tell/ she wants to cry.

I step away/ decide/ to walk up Polk/ then swing by the park/ after that/ I'll call it a night/ I go spinning a poem in my head/ hoping to will away/ the two headed demon/ that springs out of the night/ when grief is twinned with desire / madness grows wings/ and takes to the sky/ singing an aria of love/ to the dead/ I drag behind me.

Henry David Thoreau

Mitchell Zeftel

Yes, I knew, in
all her disguises, solitude.

They read me, yet I
was the stranger. I
loved the woods, but never
had the temerity to bless them
because for me, being there
was hard living, and so I
swept floors, and learned
what the dawn was, and
was in my time, a prisoner,
which is also good.

But now I have come
back, just to warn
you that I abhor a
country where 10 million
read me and where I am the stranger.

I went to Harvard Yard
and burned ten books on
structuralism and prayed in
silence, because silence
is also worthy.

Start your reading
and make your budgets

and go it alone.
Find something simple, and nurture it
Kill your cars and ban
your televisions.

I shall ascend with the
simplest sparrow, over the
pond that you're too
spoiled ever to love.

Chapter 5

Wanted in Land of Death

R. Hoodlum

Cuz or Cous... in. I been loosin ouzin
choozin noosin, death... BAD. I
had to clutch the pen weapon...
And EXPOSE REPOSE the choosin
bros who keep on. the rad
Some of the times Are Just
And some these times ARE SAD
thru them All I am Glad to
Remember... And to keep on

Hyde Street O.G.s

RaMu Aki

Hyde Street O.G.s
give no quarter
never retreat
O.G's still Gs
Thugs 4 Life, not
flippin' out trippin' w/a
gun or a knife, but
Grand Meisters of Game
down here where Game is life

bobbin' & weavin'
playin' & playin'
experts at every subtle
in & out ripple of personality
& hidden identity out here where
everything ain't hardly
what it seem

hardened to the jungle's
concrete sidewalked streets
& steel & glass cage penitentiaries
yet tenda enuff to the uprising
young Gs

professors in the virtual
classroom of reality these
O.G.s teach by example
living as they play they

run every risk—turn every turn &
twist every twist
side-by-side w/young G playa's
night-by-night
day-by-day, taking time to
represent, point out advise—
show the way

toe-to-toe w/the man, O.G.'s
even more persistent than
guerilla revolutionaries
Original Gangstas
lifelong Thugs who bring
rough honor to the name

death-before-dishonor
no-sell-out
deep knowledge of their craft
hard respect for their trade and
sharp-eyed, steel-nerved
love for the Game
fast play, smooth break &
getaway
& underneath all the beloved
neighborhood community

known personalities
passionately caught up
the danger is real of still
gettin' popped
another charge
another bit, & yet

soon's they get
back to the world
u know u gonna find
Hyde Street O.G.'s—
triumphant like president
& potentates & kings—

advanced Game facilitators
bringing balance & calm
with experience-wise
 strategies to the never-ending Game

back on Hyde St.

Kala's Feast

Ethan Davidson

1. Kala Chackra

Warm and tender multi-colored orbs
Throb with a dull and silent ache.
From where discernment's knife has cut.
The specks of blind and lustful life unformed
No longer rushing towards the gates of birth.
The wheels of suffering for them have stopped.
But other wheels remain.
    Desire presses forth to no avail
Attaching on to every passing form
And grasping at every sweet and bitter dream.
    But one can draw great power from a wound.
Like Cybel's daughters dancing on the streets
The fluids dripping crimson down their thighs.
Tears and screams mixed with the wine and ghee.
    The chariots crawl slowly down the city streets
Crushing those who blunder in their way.
The wheels press on every cobblestone
And heedlessly they crush the drunkard's feet

2. Cybel's Feast

For some the wounds remain after the feast is done.
When dogs have eaten all the scraps of meat.
    Their bodies bare reminders of the flutes and drums.
As ravens scrape their claws across the streets.
    Some burned their eyes by staring at the mid day sun.
Some hung by hooks suspended from a tree.
Some let themselves be nailed to a wooden cross
While others drank their wine and ate their ghee.
    Some soaked themselves for days inside an icy stream.
Some offered up their flesh to hungry cats.
Some pressed their sharpened knives against the wheels of life
While wine and melted butter flowed from vats.
    While Shiva threw his trident in the river's mud.
While Krishna took his throne and broke his flute.
While Kali stopped her dance and hung her tongue in shame.
While Adam walked in silence from his fruit.
    While tears and blood and milk dropped from the
smooth black stones.
While wolves grew tired of screaming at the moon.
While Hanuman ripped up his flesh down to the bones.
For one can draw great power from a wound.

The Wish

Norm Milstein

I wish to be
Beyond this land of ghosts,
Beyond foolish devotion,
Beyond mistrust,
Beyond my imperfections,
Beyond grief,
Beyond pain and the fear of pain,
Beyond the memory of human cruelty,
Beyond everything, but the accumulated beauty
Of love's most artful dreams.

Direction

William Bowden

Often I feel that
I alone am without
destination as bodies
rush this way and that
striding purposefully towards
whatever it is, long ago
forgotten.

Their eyes appear set
on true, rational goals
embarked on a journey
to a real place
towards fulfillment
as I watch from
a bench in the bus station,
skirting the crowd
on the pier, alone in the eye
of the hurricane
praying for a reason
to take that step
in any direction
wandering like a stray
in the stampede
of humanity.

Poor Playground

Melissa Newman

Dodging duck shit, obstacles in my way.
Geese bark and hiss.
Vapors of stench rise from the water.
Dead fish rot and stink.
Young men fish, casting their lines in the shallow.
Spent lures hang on utility wire.
Old men in motorized wheelchairs lust after women with legs.
Wrinkled faces suck oxygen between puffs, seeking breath to speak.
Chorus wanders the grounds, whispering, giggling, presenting.
Young love embraces under shelter unaware.
Politics and coffee as usual convenes nearby.
Tamping, raking dust on the diamond vibrates in the distance.
Mound of mulch, cedar scent long gone, begs me to take it.
Porta-potty in the walkway shows they tried?
Black boxes belch the music no one cares for.
Curious tiny trailer, what does he do in there?
Pussy willows have spilled their guts to the swamp.
Dry leaves move together, whispering summer secrets.
Dodging duck shit, obstacles in my way.
Geese bark and hiss.

Cockroach Dreams

Joel Fallon

Wake. Stretch,
Try to remember
fragments of a dream.

As always, dream fragments
scuttle away like cockroaches
in sudden light—

Hurry, scurry into
linoleum cracks
of a cheap motel.

A dream worth remembering
can become the soul of a poem.
What is the trick to recall dreams?

Dim the light,
liquefy your gaze,
look at something else.

Then,
out of the corner of your eye
a slight movement

the timid cockroach dream
that may become
the soul of a poem.

Return of the Dream Girl

Garrett Murphy

He lay face-down, unwilling to move in the darkness about him. He wanted desperately to twist into a fetal position, but had not even the motivation to do so. Nothing he had done seemed to matter anymore; all efforts had been quashed and all seemed lost. Nothing to do but to close one's eyes and wait.

He felt something push against his neck—a jab, a nudge or shove? Decided to ignore it, thinking he was hallucinating—

"Hey." (Not from his mouth.)

—but the sensation continued– increasingly forceful but never

violent. Rather benevolent authority, this was–but again, this was hardly an officer's jackboot pushing on his neck. He turned to see what little he could.

The glint of patent leather and of a bit of metallic trim along the heel—he saw a woman's foot, clad in a black classic pump, peeking from what appeared to be a jet-black evening gown that went down to just below her ankle; from what he could see of the heel he could tell it was at least five inches.

Before he could grasp this, she tucked her foot under his head and pushed it upwards, forcing him to look up at her.

"Remember me? You had me up on your bedroom wall, in many daydreams...even..." He gasped involuntarily at another jab, this time in his crotch. "—in a few *wet dreams*!"

"Don't worry," she went on, "I'm not here to hurt you. Tease you, a little... but you did crave this once upon a time, remember."

He had to admit he still did—he felt himself aroused at her caress of his genital area; though her shoe was potentially dangerous, she was making sure not to hurt him.

Taking action, he kissed the toe of her left foot and ran his hands along it, massaging the sinews while her right foot massaged his pubic area. Though still very dark, he had no trouble locating anything, indeed, the only thing lost was his melancholia.

She kicked his neck up, forcing him to sit up, and sat herself down to face him.

"Remember, all is not as lost as it seems. Should you ever feel it is—" She wrapped her arms around him and embraced him. "—just recall me, my fan."

He returned her embrace, relieved by her presence.

He woke up to a new morning, fully alert, and out of the depression he had been in when he had retired last night. Things had to start anew, he realized.

About to rise, he looked to his right and was shocked at the sight of a black classic pump next to his face.

Sitting up to fathom that, he noted there was something under his blanket between his legs. Pushing them aside, he saw another classic pump. Patent leather—five-inch heel. Looking closely, he realized they were even the same size as hers.

He would not be depressed for quite some time.

Letters To Another Human Like Me

H.D. MOE

Bugged by fairies, I can overhear the spheres on the juke box of the poli-universe what came around always new turned back to its makings & invented it anew too. Nothing remains the same. Different empty shapes appear though for those, who enjoy these protean abysses, contemplating a quiet between the wiry traffic, the sudden floods of sentiment rushing through. These underlooking animisms show their glow from any part of me that isn't clothed & rays shoot out mathematical angles of my body so that I may not disrobe myself in the presence of anyone it seems for they always think my flesh is nuclear, I'm the devil, an invented zombie or I have arrived from another planet than this one, or some such nonsense. Even shaking hands or hugging anyone becomes impossible unless I cover myself completely like a traditional Muslim woman. Whenever I leave my hut I carry in a knapsack a hooded robe, mask & gloves to don when I reach the outskirts of the village. The other creatures who visit me & I meet along the way, are not put off by my glowing rays at all, in fact, they cheerfully greet me on my walks through the woods & console me with their songs, chirps & voices, at down-in-the-dumps times I feel from being rejected by my own kind. Earlier, I wished that the fairies & their emanations would leave me but now I would feel greatly impoverished if either the magical winged ones inside me or their rays & glows did go, in spite of the resulting alienation I suffer from being shunned & vilified by my fellow human beings. Not only am I continually enlightened by the deep gossip humming & musically proclaiming throughout my listening brain, all matter of friendly phantoms, duppies, elves & tricksters from the past, future & everywhere now, it seems, are drawn by these emanations & along with the birds, bears, panthers, foxes & hares (to name a few) they talk & gesture to me wonderful strange but true informations. Did you know that truth is not in the idealizations of demonstrative & experimental science or any known discipline? Truth is the unknowing that's always new. It's not even in what I'm or rather the fairies, ghost creatures & animals are saying here. It could only be whatever it is, in the vast intimacy of you & the creative poli-universe or maybe coming novelly from some whiteheadian creative baby god or goddess at the nub & circumference of every where always. I don't know & am not being told by these cogent posits swimming up to & throughout me. If I do get even an improvised guess, I tell you or whoever's open to my inklings. Meanwhile, hidden in the midst of unnecessary biases & hardships & the wars resulting from this lack of caring vision, sequestered in my little cabin deep in the forest here, away also from the prominent robot-like thinking of my species, although without the companionship & love of another human, awash with intelligences of nature & illuminating, loving, numinous spirits of the real nether world, I'm happily jumping to an undefeated dance.

Mirror Buildings

John Delaney

Mirror buildings
capturing light

Mirror buildings
painted with glass

Mirror buildings
cracked with pain

Reflect a shattered fist
of the working class

Acropolistic architecture
a distant democracy glistens

The tops
like push-pins
stick through clouds
Alexander would be proud

Plate my world silver
and paint my heart blue
push them further
into the sky

As it grows dark
I close my eyes
I can see the sun
no more

It started ...

Debra Turner

It started
like the sand
coming out from under my feet.
I knew I should move,
back up, go forward, but I couldn't.
I just stood there:

HOMELESSNESS
Then I got outplaced,
replaced, let go, fired.
Then time sped up
and it slowed down.
The months came faster,
the money went faster.
I moved out and into my car.
I thought if I could just
wake up one morning and feel better
I could fit the pieces back together
and get ahead and out of the hole I'd fallen into,
while I was just standing still
and everything was slower and faster and farther and
    nowhere.

CANNOT HAPPEN TO ME
I never thought
this would happen to me
because I just wouldn't let it.
I was too smart and too far along toward getting ahead.

BECAUSE I WILL NOT LET IT

Tall Talk, Part Two
Dedicated to William Norwood and Jenny Wiley

Utah Carol

Pretty is as pretty does.

Do not pull it out if you do not have the qualifications to use it.

Sometimes you are the Louisville Slugger, sometimes you are the ball.

Good looks is one thing, sex appeal is all things.

Patience is not a question of time. Patience is a question of faith.

Never walk through a doorway with your mouth open, your money in your hand, your pants down around your ankles, or your dress up over your head.

Never count the money in your pocket. It has already been spent.
Count your next money as best as you can.

The only thing worse than working is being broke.

It is more important to learn than it is to teach, but always remember all real teachers were students.
A good student sits down, learns his lessons,
does his homework and becomes a professional.

Six P's: Proper planning prevents piss poor performance.

Do not lie to yourself.

Your ears do not receive when your mouth is transmitting.

Do not pay anybody to do what you can do yourself.

What Better Cover

DIAMOND DAVE WHITTAKER

What better cover
for the murder
of the sons
and daughters of light
down
through
history
than a church
that claims to speak
in His name

Dancing sideways
down the ribbon of time
the path ahead lit
by the echo behind

The past shakes hands
with the future
through the now
right now

Sometimes I see myself
walking through the sky
just living on Rainbow time

Bottle Pickers

Jan Steckel

"I felt violated," says our new neighbor
after seeing someone go through her trash.

An old woman in a coolie hat
forages through our cans.
I bring the bottles left in the house.
She takes them with knobby hands
and a dried-apple wrinkled smile.

Another day while I'm out walking,
an old lady's rickety bottlecart loses a wheel.
I twist a paper clip, pin the wheel back on.
She smiles, nods over hands pressed together.
I can't tell if she's the same one who was in
     front of our house.
The ancient cart pushing ladies
all look alike to me.

I know they're not all the same
because sometimes I see them cross paths,
hear them greet each other
in up-and-down tones I can't understand.
They stop talking when I approach.
Their seamed faces crack into grins.
They wave as though to an idiot child.

I don't feel violated.
I feel blessed.

I Should Tell You About Desert Varnish

Keith Walker

1.
This invitation to the desert reminds me of lives
lost in real estate comedy
a vein of borax sifted through lace curtains in Trona,
safe deposit box of the great Mojave desert
a gypsum mine dust bin
where all muckers breathe in cadence

2.
Without a reservation the desert can appear
Crowded out here that is:
sandstone rivulets devoid of caution
retreat along creosote washes
the crucible of mojave quartz, mosaic canyons, slick rock,
desert varnish
sparks thrown to the wind
I am inclined to seek an elixir which will embrace
even the teeth rotting sugars found here

3.
A search party or disoriented vulture out of calcite canyon
under orange tarps and wild turkey
jokes undulate above the chalk into bright hazelike distemper
my fever at its highest
and out there in the mirage, nothing
not even the desert dogs are stirring
and in this precise moment,
I decide to move on through Garlock
declaring the bikes on standdown,
leaving them to their spinning and flashing in the oasis

Sun, Sun, Sun

DON BRENNAN

You are my sun sun sun, sing woman
Lady of the day on the noonday street
Sunshine you are

Silk voice, long print dress, flowery
Slate wavy hair
Old black woman singing backed up
Amped up sunshine

Old white man sitting on the noonday
Sidewalk in a drizzling rain
Guitar amped, woman leaning down
Into that guitar sound

You are my sun sun sunshine man
Guitar man, propped up on your oxygen tank,
Plastic tube feeding your nose

Old man
Old woman
Her raining down her light up smile
all over him

Starting to rain for real now
Playing, singing, now she laughs

You you you
Sun sun sun
Are my sunshine.

We Blame the Pirate

ZACH KARNAZES

We blame the pirate,
The **hustler** the **pimp**
The **street vendor I** bought headphones from

                              Because **we never learned** economics
                                  I don't know what is a
                                      dividend or hedgefund

but I know the **seas aren't plundered** by pirates or ex-prisoners
they are **poisoned** by **fine-speaking** gentlemen
that have good reputations and wear Armani
successful enterprise of names like **BP and Chevron**
A pirate takes my wallet but an
                    oil spill
                          lasts
                              an aeon.

The Hustler does petty gambling,
slangin dope and **serving time**
in a prison where he makes clothes
for **twenty dollars** on the dime
where he is **raped and beaten**
while prison guards **ignore the screams**
now what's the real crime?
Who **calls the shots** and plans the schemes?

The Pimp will sell a woman
whose husband died in Iraq
now she's a widow
to a **politician** who *votes* **for war**
and **buys her love** behind tinted limo windows

The Vendor is a fence for headphones that were stolen
cannot afford the rent **since he was displaced** out of Oakland
they won't give a black man a job
so now he **sleeps at the train station**
evicted from his apartment
to make men rich by **housing speculation**

Does the man who **steals an apple** deserve to lose his hand
because **businessmen in castles** put price tags on all the land?

Animal Limericks

Taylor Brown

KUSH

There was once a little orange kitten
Everyone who met him was smitten
    Yet his attitude showed,
    His extra-hyper mode,
And that mode showed no signs of quittin'!

SPUNKY

There once was a dog called Spunky,
Who was a little bit chunky,
    He found something gross,
    And Rolled a bit too close,
Now he smells a little funky

KARMA

Karma was a happy brown dog,
Who slept like an ill-tempered log,
    She tossed and turned,
    And quickly learned
That a bed is what she loved to hog.

TANK

There once was a little tan dog,
Who moved as much as a cog,
    He fought a small kitten,
    Ran in circles, was bitten,
And then slept as sound as a log.

Dog, In Golden Gate

VICKIE CIMPRICH

Last Tuesday he lurched off
alone, obedient to the atherosclerotic clot
that leashed the right half sphere
of what's behind his weather-speckled face.

His mind's teeth clamped down
on somebody else's cell phone
and shook it so a social worker at General
would protect his pending SS status,
and he could flop down at last
on an indoor bed.

Oh farewell home-pen lofty cables,
farewell moon over Sharon Meadow,
where Dog lent his salt to bench and bush!

Cronies, salute with grin or rabbit punch
this brown bag mead mate of many seasons.

Goodbye Cookie Lady,
charmed for the last time
into Planter's cracker-pack-and-dry-sock
offerings.

Dog rounded his corner
and the sirens caged him.

Three Short Poems About Work

Sanford Dorbin

Graveyard Shift
Dustmopping the floor
she reaches for a piece of dirt.
It turns into a moth and stutters away.

Manual Labor
The kind of job where you
have to wash your hands before you pee.

Timber
Squat as a miner, he fit like a salamander
into the hillside, unmoved by the hum & shriek
of his machine as he cut, dropping trees like enemies
and opening holes in the earth — both of which bothered
but kept him. Working the bole of a chinquapin
one morning in icy rain, he slipped backward down a slope
in the middle of a cut, wrenching free & throwing
his chainsaw like a pilot's canopy aside as he went
skidding along the clay-mud earth. Another day
high up a dead live oak, he lost a tied-off round & hollered
before it landed a foot from the feet of the man
grounding for him, splintering a wooden walkway
beside. They exchanged glances concise as telegrams
and continued the job, swimming in the sweat of present time.

Chapter 6

I Am a Street Performer

John Duke

i am a street performer at the wharf
a fishermen's delight in san francisss
co-dependent like the families plan to morph
they're loving everybody as it isss

so give me money now or else i cry
when i go home but not in front of thy
for if you see me in decrepit mode
my future happiness it does not bode

so i am here to get some bucks and that
is why i'm here and this is where i'm at
i came here with the thought that i would grow
but after this rejection i don't know

at least i came and showed the world my stuff
i stayed and played and laid it out enough

On the Street

JACQUI

Just sitting out there by the
library ...could have been you
or I reading the paper, scanning
the news headlines. Though he was
intently reading every word,
like he had all the time in
the world. Just sitting
there relaxing in
the warm noonday sun
with his bare
feet propped
up on resting
on a soiled,
rolled up
gray blanket

I am from a place ...

JoJo

I am from a place ...
Where I hide behind my own skin.
A place where I run away from my own feelings
    and never like to face the truth.
Knowing how to live and yet struggling with life.

I am from a place ...
A place where I see people laying down in the streets
    asking for food or money.
A place where people fight just over a type of color.

I am from a place ...
A place that at a young age had to experience adult life.
A place where I was fighting to survive with out any food.

I am from a place ...
A place where I was made fun of for my sexuality.
A place where I would get beaten up by other students.

I am from ...
A place where I got neglected by real parents.
A place where I would be left by myself at home.
where I would move from house to house.

I am from a place ...
where I've gotten adopted at the age of six ...
A place where I got put in group homes because
    my parents couldn't take care of me.

I am from a place …
A place where now I know what I want to do with my life.
A place where people are helping me to get my life on track.
A place with positive encouragement.

I am from a place where I could write about my feelings
          on a piece of paper and share them.

This is where I am from.

Gossip

Gloria Rainwater

To gossip is to kill a soul
First the other's, then one's own
It will never make you whole
It will burn inside you like a stone.

Gossip is a way to feel superior
Competing all the while you make someone inferior
While doing it you don't have to see your own flaws
Perhaps that is the real cause.

There's nothing more damaging to community
Than picking on someone to achieve immunity
If you want to be able to look at yourself in the
	mirror
Do behavior that will bring people near.

To criticize only creates separation
The real challenge is cooperation
It bridges the invisible distance between us all
Which never really existed in the first place, after all.

On the Death of Whitney Houston

Marsha Campbell

Heart's knowing is
    how to recover from loss
    how to believe
    and how to balance one's energy
when another being has been
    run out of breath
    drained of heartbeats
    claimed by an early sleep
        for a star to enter darkness

Heart's knowing is
    a confession of drugs
        mixed with alcohol
    an early sleep
    a lesson in how to dream with awareness
    how to dream in sleep and sleep in dream

    so that the soul becomes articulate

Wheel of War
Signs At The National Democratic Convention, 1968, In Chicago, Illinois

Janell Moon

LAY YOUR BODY ON THE LEVER OF THE WAR MACHINE
GIVE PEACE A CHANCE
END OPPOSITION TO WOMEN
WE HAVE THE RIGHT TO MARRY
COPS OUT OF GHETTO
SMASH ROTC
SOLDIERS HOME SAFE
CALL Laura, SDS, 826-2744
BOYCOTT WESTINGHOUSE
Because the poison air is hot and choking
PEANUT BUTTER BETTER THAN POT
Because chunks of him die as he shoots
Because his first kill, young farmer
Because chunks of him die as he shoots
Because he is alone in this field
Because he thinks only to live
FLOWERS AND FLAMES
Because a mother sees the American wearing her son's clothes
and knows
Because there is no preparing for the smell
Because there are 18 year olds ordered to play God

The soldier returns to American soil in only fifteen hours. Two hours after landing, he eats dinner with his family who tell him about the garden they planted. After lunch, he takes a Budweiser out back to be by himself and sees the carrots and pole beans.

Darkness to clear skies over San Francisco, over the Golden Gate, down to San Jose and a loop to turn back to Oakland. Babylift descends with babies in 2 foot square cardboard boxes strapped down the center of the plane. The Red Cross workers tell the toddlers they will arrive soon at their new country, and the Vietnamese children who are old enough call, *Amerika, Amerika.*

OWN VISION It's like in Vietnam, you see what you saw and you carried it like a seed that grew in you, couldn't touch it, couldn't eat it, but it was there. I personally knew no one who was drafted. My husband, father, brother-in law were deferred for their professional jobs. My brother for mental incapacity. Poor healthy kids went as heroes and returned with war engrained in minds and bodies, some still begging thirty years later near where I have my office. They repeat, always repeat the rubber boat they sat in alone in the swamp. Some together, now gone. The boat they used for a roof at night. Or nights in a tree when they held on to the branch with both hands. Our pilots bombed targets, just followed the topographical abstract landscape so pretty from a distance. They didn't escape either. Light and water met the eye in a rainbow, but any rainbow here was a fluke of nature, and they knew it. No one won, if we are talking human. Go to Church, Sanchez, Noe, or Castro Street in San Francisco. There's an old vet at each corner. They'll tell you of limbs flying, their minds rewinding. A record of sun burnt things along with the smiles for money.

KIND DOCTOR My brother didn't go to Vietnam. *Flat feet*, the doctor said. Besides, he doesn't eat rice or lettuce, beans. *Diet too narrow*, the doc wrote, stamping him UNFIT and leaving him free to chase his hallucinations.

ART MUSEUM JUNKIES We stare at the closed theatre curtain. My mother owns a drapery shop, so we sit and figure out the yards. What a sale! The curtains open. It's dead on arrival. The spotlight shone a brilliant yellow; then a camera's distance to black and white. What an absence. Douglas Gordon videos show veiled lettering on walls. An old woman who sits in the center row yells to the audience, "A moment's silence," for someone close to her. Why in San Francisco do we clean off graffiti? Muni sprayed with outlined messages of SHRED LIFE and WIPER BOY and WAR TOY. Who knows what the letters speak. PANTY WANTY. In my ghetto, we talk swag gestures and tape measures.

Poor Man on the Street

Delia Tomino Nakayama

standing here on the corner
apart from the excited crowds
some might stop and pay me attention
and give me due
while most are uncaring and distracted
by the whims of the day
i might drink a beer
i might smoke a cigarette
i have holes in my clothes
but a penny in my pocket
but least i know what i am
and what i ain't

On the Shoulders of the Dead

Deirdre Evans

We wander each in our own dreams.
Our dreams merge and parts
Merge and cling together
Dreaming, each one of us, separately
for our unique separate selves
Dreaming of coming together
with other dreamers who dream
the same Big Dream that we do
A dream of diversity encouraged
within a peaceful world where
each one of us is allowed to follow
our path and develop our talents to
our greatest capacity
Each following one's own true will while
harming none
Another impossible dream? Sure!
Glittering with fairy dust
wrapped well in the undulating rings
of Neptunian illusion, delusion, fusion
not fission is an important mission
impossible? Maybe, but how can we know
until we try. Our world of unthinkable
blessings and horrors of technology
the offspring of Humanity
Salvation or Insanity waits
in the void—We do not walk
We are carried on the sturdy, sure
shoulders of our Wise and Mighty Dead.

Second Hand

Fay Small

When young I seldom got anything new, never had a bike or a doll, scarcely had anything. In high school, a classmate owned five sweaters. It was hard to believe that someone had so many sweaters. I only had one.

During World War II, I won a scholarship to Brooklyn College and wanted a watch. My father said, "No, a war bond instead." Pleading finally got my way. We rode the subway to the Bowery, on the lower east side of Manhattan, to buy a watch. My father met a friend who said, "Don't buy a watch. It is too expensive. Wait until the end of the war." My heart dropped. Thinking on my feet, I said, "Poppa, I must have a watch. The professor said, as a science major, you need a watch with a second hand to time the experiments." For science, Poppa could not refuse. He bought me a watch that cost $40.00. I still have it and it still keeps good time.

While attending school, I did my homework on the dining room table, always dreaming of a desk of my own. When my sons got married, I inherited their desks. Do I use them? I still write on my dining room table.

My father was a tailor and had a used clothing store. He bought old clothes, like Simon Ackerman and Three G's, and restored them. I remember carrying bundles of clothes on the trolley car, at a cost of three cents, from my home in Williamsburg to the weaver on Broome Street, on the lower east side of Manhattan. For a fee, holes were rewoven. The customers loved my father. I can still hear them calling, "Pa, do you have anything for me?" He saved them a lot of money. For nine or ten dollars they could own a fine quality suit. Is it any wonder that I like to buy at flea markets, buying old dolls and restoring like new?

Lost Fathers
for Marsha

Anna Sears

The fathers we have lost are always missing
and some part of us remains
the age we were when they disappeared.

Why don't we get it together, people wonder
(sometimes aloud and in our presence)
why haven't we done more?

Actually, for a child of four
or a child of six
we are doing well.

Unseen tear in the heart
still stings.

Passover Scene
Civic Center, San Francisco

Jack Hirschman

Wearing a large blue
and silver-fringed blanket
over his head and jacket
and down around his shoulders
a homeless man peers
into a garbage can
for some scraps to eat,
finds nothing with his eyes,
reaches in and rummages
but still finds nothing
and so continues to the next
street's garbage can
on this Passover a dream
of matzoh in a desert
synonymous with bread.

Maw

Denis Calin

Depthless voids above me
Striking deep,
And thickly sky was rolling
Down to crush my soul.
They didn't want me in the pit
The heaven also, having checked
My papers sent my ass go crawling
Up the streets
Of Tenderloin. Of the moonlit
Undersoil stations all the drugs
I've tasted and the grime I've seen.
A desperate situation
Some might spare a quarter
Others yet—some weed,
But money's never been
An issue, I only smoke
Red Chesterfield.
The moon within me
Rises full and beastly,
Animalistic, gnostic and sincere,
O heavens laugh, o holes of hell
Will count my statistic—
The mother wolf is going for the kill.

Closer Than You Think ...

Tom Odegard

If you stand real close,
close to anyone U.S.A. you'll feel their heat,
close to a building away from the street
so gathered together you'll get less wet.
All the while keep your eyes down to your feet
and your mouth tight so the words don't speak
and your rage and grief can boil in your belly
mixed with some port you'll keep overnight.
And if you crimp tight
hold your shoulders back and your butt taut
your legs'll be stiff while your chest sticks out
so you won't get grief and you might get food
'cause we learned this shit as babes in the wood.
That's right kids,
how to stay dry, hot, and frightful in the scary-hood.
It's all an act, a jive, a strut, a way of being
that soon stands in for a life we call uptight living.

From Turk St to Market following Hyde
you'll pass a dozen people who are pushin' their pride
standing close, eyes downcast, crimped uptight
doing their homeless, impoverished American duty.
WhaddidIsay? Poverty's an American necessity?
You betchersweetass my friend
it's America's true bottom line
as necessary as apple pie
as well as that mythic cream puff: Mom

Back to the Street

George Wynn

The City of Shame is closing
down the Self Help Center
on Turk Street
the workers care for
the people in the Tenderloin
they call them
by their first name
where will the workers
—once homeless—go?
where will their
client-friends go?

the city workmen
on their sweeping machines
zigzagging the street
—do they care about the Tenderloin?
—would they die for the Tenderloin?
the men in blue racing
through the Tenderloin
on a bust
—do they care about you
in the Tenderloin?
—would they kill for the Tenderloin?

bureaucratic gamesters
hone their knives
and cut Tenderloin throats
damn shame
they put all the blame
on the deficit
but we'll never
forget the politicos
who took a walk
down cop-out alley

Vision of The End

O.D. LUDYEH (BERNIE SULLIVAN)

    fierce fight i
           my ne'er weary fearsome foe   aloft

           i dare goad
                across my dropped acres
      of scare dross.

   but, o'er four decades of diligent suds drub
       (for "her" hands sans haste)
the washer wench at the ford   must soak and soap the stench
      scrub to blench the bloody wast
   from the sole worth
       of earth's birth sheath's war-ripped duds'
role
       then hush-a-bye wring the thrust-
swing
  from my torture-tasted torment tested
soul.
    hang my once   **braggart and swaggart,**
    yet now sulking   **and skulking breath**
from the chief   of the gangs   **of gag**
lines
   that sag 'tween   **the open-close**
poles

of my multiply divided 'gainst itself   mind.
   to permit its eyelets to drip cry to   death
sigh(ze).

sins of scorpion pins   cinch   the stubbed toes of **this**
life
that   "she"   wrung-hung-stole **to**
cold

                  my flesh flaunts scores of
sores,
   scads of prick-picked and knife nicked scabs,
a scarlet-grand skin scape   of a barge of brand-iron
scars.
   though my cement monument head
                          (oft snubbed from below the
belt,
   else slugged by abash love, sash hate hell
above)

   dangles pinches of hourglass sand o'er the plot
         where-in my   grr!rough   ruffled
my   (dis)gust-rusted   once   shape   must   rot,

   a wreath reeking of repeat e'er more effete
retreats
and wreaked by ignoble ignominious defeats
         —a scraping scraplet chaplet i dread
      even all of me stone bone dead—

```
d e c k s        m       y
b r o k e n               n e
ver
   a                   n
       o a   k    e    n      neck.
```

note: (the tradition of the washer (woman) at the ford
          —the vision of one's imminent death—
          laces Celtic literature and folklore)

Why I Didn't Make the Russian River Trip

Dave Roams

Why I didn't make
the Russian River trip—
Walked by Leona's
Heard a hustler's
Shrieking laugh
Drank a Scotch River.

you get to walk
[done long before knowing the concept of the practice(s)]

QRHANDJR

    you get to walk   with
    the stalkers   and   that
    ain't gonna be easy

    you got to   walk
    with the stalkers   do we
    really   see what we   here

    hear   whose foot steps   whose
    folk steps   and   ever present
    where(s)   and   you   there

    with out friends   all ways a lone
    and   one of them   to them   just
    another   another stalker   hearing

    what you hear   too   a perfect circle
    hiding lethal imperfection(s)

    the lay of the land
    not just the 'loin
    the big amerika joint   and
    not the kind you smoke

    security needed
    all over the place(s)
    picking pockets   and
    you could be one of them   to

another   which them   which
another   no exit   no entrance
there is here   now   shopping   and
hustling for need(s)   now

flags flying every where(s)   (a) big
sale(s)   how easily radios talk paranoia(s)
business as usual(s)   globally a bargain
usuals as business   compared to what(s)

if you get(s)   there   on time   be
tween the throbbing   pay master(s)

you shudder coming   and   going from
the each of   the many   cross towning(s) be
tween bus   taxi   foot patrol(s)   a stroll
is suspicious   knowing   and   guessing

whose capabilities are up   for grab(s)   which
them   which an other   no exit   no entrance
there is here   now   moving   with shopping bags
is there a way home   here   if you're lucky enough

to have a question like that   will you make it
this time   now   looking like a terrorist   look(s)
not just an other   stalker   the kind that might
who's got their hands full   of what(s)   could contain

explosive(s)   more than santeria candles
picturesque(s)   and   quaint caribbean dolls   each
with a rain bow of pins   placed in vital spots   that
person scoping you   thought(s) crazy with detail(s)   circuitry

could be used to make infernal device(s)   and you know
them   and   what the one who's doing   the fantastic look
out(s)   probably thinks a short list   too short for comfort(s)
what might be   a factor   and   you've got your keys in

the easy to get to pocket   hoping you can catch the second
half   kick off   kick back   chomp on the rye crackers   and   brie
sip some red ale   just an other walk with thee done   just an other
lucky not to be a woman   or   a child   these steps take place

you get to walk
with

Chapter 7

Weather

WARREN

Does the wild wind not call the trees
Without knowing the effect it will have?
Does the nightingale now call to the blue
Moon without purpose?
Is not every mind of humanity robbed
Of the sweet innocence given at birth?
Spirits speak to me.
The voices of ancestors forgotten
Glide in and out of tree of land
Not touched for nigh a hundred years.
The dead linger in places where light
Is sought out, love only occurs
When hate cannot.
Yet somehow worlds avoid colliding
In a perfect world there might
Be peace. But yet what is peace really
Except the dull grayness of a blackboard
Uniform and always the same,
Complete and total equality is rich
And amusing, for think of the great
American Condor forced to walk
Because of its massive wingspan and
How it dwarfs the poor swallow.
In light of recent events we
Have to realize that equality
Will only bring defeat and the earth
Shall crumble away beneath us
And rain into the cold depths
Of space.

Before Cats Walked

J. MICHAELS

A silent place in
   the mind,
  fatigue,
   it's good to have a best friend,

one that
  acts like it wants
  the fellowship
  the kinsmanship,

just the being around when the telephone
   laughs its

long, monotone jelly roll into a cold, lonely ear.

If friendship were to sail
  for friendlier shores.

Where would the fatigue and the silent
      place
  connect?

Ah, they are always at
   home with a quiet man,

choosing nothing but his bed and
   the
     darkness.

He is willing to call these brothers to
        him, always.

The Talk About Grace

Sheppard Benet Kominars

"Dearie, slip
off your es-
padrilles and I'll
tell you all about Grace."

"Christ,
it's hot; here's
a beer,
I think
it's cold enough.
How long is it
since we came off
from those bulls of ours
for a moment's peace?"

"And if you
don't think
you've said
the truth, Chu-Chu,
cop this!
He won't
let it
chance to heal
before he's on it
again."

"I
don't know

what to do
if he keeps going
for it
the way he does.
You
know, I
can get a
cancer?"

"They
are something!
Just look
at this. What
were you
coming
to tell me
about Grace?"

"She's
left Harry
again;
this one's a
Marine.
What he sees
in her
I'll never know,
even with her
real teeth;
and you
should see him
buyin' Sen-sen
at Louie's place
Saturday night;
with those uni-

forms you
can see every-
thing he's
packin'
her in with."

"She always was
that kind. —
Harry's a
dear all these
years
puttin' up with her;
every time another
crotch passes
she's off
again
like the diarrheas.
Besides what
you can see
bulgin' —
what's in
a uni-
form anyway!"

"Dearie,
cross yourself
when you say
the truth."

The Heart of Things

Paul Drabkin

Anything can be a poem
if, finding the right angle
you unearth the hidden heart.
Then the artichoke, too,
will have its say, even as you
remove each successive leaf
scraping the surface with your teeth
and tossing what's left over
on the compost heap:
some day you may discover
that you've somehow fertilized the
past
which has always been under the skin
of everything you ever touched.

Flowers for an Old Man

DAVID SCHOOLEY

•The beard earth•

Crumpled by his cart
    An old man fallen
Startled in his only
    Journey infinite
Under the plaza trees
    An old man dying.
Nothing known to them
    In rattled darkness blind
Of this fearful light,
    Giant stars in his beard.

    Mercy has a human heart.

In this raucous time of no flowers
When safer men must needs cleave frailty
    It seems
Having left that old man on the street
    To die
I plead with you for once reveal
The delicate blue veined petals of
    Your fear.

In the Metro

Ronald F. Sauer

a regular day
and grateful for it
a day in sync with divinity…
Some thirty yards ahead of her
heading into the Metro
and turning around to look at her,
thinking, yes, that's right:
she's a movie star,
some goddess fresh from Fellini.
How lucky I am to have
a panther, a genius, and
more dependable than diamonds
and finer than the stars,
and to think she loves me.
It makes me juicy with the light.

Trent
To Trent Hayward aka Harpo Corlene who died on the street June 2, 2000

Jess (Ben) Clarke

Bent to that
demon wind
blowing from within
and without

without a home
curled tight to the needle,
cops slide you in to the
bag like you weren't.

Man,
you were a great voice whose
words we so badly need
to hear
here
—haven't got enough
words
to cover this hole in my gut

feel it rotting too,
one step behind you
buddy man.
I don't want us to go there
all of us
togetheralone
narcotizing
the painjoy
of fearsuccess.

was it the shadow of doug's
rescue?
celebrity charge to the front page
and outside
the paper
lying on cement
you're dead.

Trent man,
why you went out that way
curled round the needle
on the street—no back
flat on it and hurting
medicated in to no-land
other land
over

blue land blurry blue of better wombs
I can't dare to cross it
I'm burnin' blurry here.

I remember the way you transcribed that interview
getting it down word by word word for word
but I don't know the sound of the tape that was running
inside you at the brink of extinct
link to who we really are

Margot says you wouldn't have died like that in Cuba

no homeless heroin/heroes bunked down on concrete

I remember the way you packed that pack every night
—loading a tome from the library—was it Whitman?—after
a day of pecking words on our whizbangnew G4
speedsters
while you sleep out
while you sleep out.

Fucking city without.

Demon wind without
10,000 out
everynight out
staying warm with blankets,
booze, needles and shared stories

Trent
you told us story—your granddad in his crazy cave with the
carvings
how can you be gone?
You can't be gone.
You are still here inside me
making me look at my demons
that could kill me slowly
or quickly.

Joaquin's Mind
Joaquin is not yet 5 years old. His mom wrote/quoted this to submit

Meg Whittaker Greene

A glimpse into the working of Joaquin's mind:

"I kiss Frankie on the head.
The kisses go through his head and enter his brain
Then they are thoughts.
He is thinking.
Then the thoughts leave his brain through his
head
                                      and enter the room.
Now they are questions.
The questions fill up the house.
When the questions are done they go back into
his head and enter his brain.
They are thoughts again.
That's what happens when I kiss Frankie. Okay?"

Brother Dream

Jerry Ratch

It's always daylight there
My brother comes running
    down the sidewalk
holding out his arms and
    calling my name
He's wearing suspenders. He's
    gotten thinner
in heaven
He embraces me warmly
wanting us to be friends
I give up trying to resist
I don't know why I ever did
in real life

If nice guys finish last

ZACK REED

If nice guys finish last,
The rat race is not worth watching.
A shoulder to lean on,
Lovecards in crayons,
that's what I'm offering.

If nice guys finish last,
the Cynics pass
for forensic Authority
Juniper kisses are stationary
In Hesitation's routine allegory.

If nice guys finish last,
The divorce rate still rises—
hearts are chiseled
since passion's embers
are charcoaled stones sleeping in white ash.

If nice guys finish last,
then George Orwell is a non-fiction poet.
Sarah Palin is a hopeless romantic.
Lawyers are Apollo and Ovids.

If nice guys finish last,
I've no need to ask your number,
what could be is for you to dream,
For younger hearts to wonder.

Eternity

Jeffery Jewelle Joseph, Jr.

V 1
> It's been an eternity
> Since our eyes met
> Now again I'll take this time to pay my respects.

V 2
> On this day I'll confess to you
> There's been someone else
> And I'm sure you would love to see me happy
> But now your soul rests.

Ch 1
> While driving down the coast
> Tears like fire in my eyes
> Memories of those who come close to me
> Either have gone away or died.

V 3
> Grass is green
> Sky so blue
> Not one cloud to be seen
> In my hand I have flowers for you
> The colors of red white and blue.

V 4
    She stands so close to me
    Reminding me of you
    Is it wrong accepting her love and devotion
    Knowing she's not you?

V 5
    Before I leave
    I'll say a prayer
    And again I shall cry
    Down on my knees hands held close to me
    My only wish is to kiss you goodbye.

Ch 2
    While driving down the coast
    Tears like fire in my eyes
    Memories of those who come close to me
    Either have gone away or died.

My Beloved Tenderloin

Kat Krieger

My beloved Tenderloin, Yes!
In all its dirtiness and neglect. The smell of urine permeates the streets

And yet the smile of one black man among many lights up my life in an instant connection of our humanity.

Parents push their little children in strollers. An old lady walks the cutest little dog who barks like a big bad pit bull.
    I feel at home.

There is the young man who watches us jam (You know: shake some tambourines, slap on some drums, pick on the guitar.) He is so innocent, sweet and shy. He has a look of happiness as he takes part by being there.
    It's good to be part of a group.

That same night he was stabbed and left for dead. Thank God, he didn't die. In a couple of days we {me and the guys who were jamming} were able to see him in the hospital. He came back to us months later healed but not the same.

The criss-crossing of race, gender orientation, generations and views on life is so natural. Nothing fake or manufactured about it.
    It's wonderful.

A Vietnamese man struggles to get up on the curb, a black woman lends him a hand. He smiles, mouths thanks as he looks her gently in the eye.

On the corner two Latinos greet me with, "Hola señorita."

A tiny Japanese lady collects cans and puts them in a large heavy sack on her back.

Magnifica! Lisa dresses to the hilt, with stiletto heels, a mini skirt and shiny top, swings her hips in a sexy walk. Her hair and makeup is perfecto! "Hi Honey," she says in the deepest horsiest voice.

Young adolescent boys whiz by me on skate boards. A Hayward law student salutes as he rides his bike down the street.

A thin, gaunt gentlemen sweeps the sidewalk in front of the "Fool's" ministry. He isn't paid to do it. He tells us he takes pride in where he stands and lives day after day.

Pure enjoyment in the presence of these wonderful people makes me feel so alive in "The Land of the Living Dead."

Helping someone across the street, carrying someone else's groceries up the stairs, giving out oranges, sharing a drink, laughter all around. These too, a part of the Tenderloin I love.

Sharing a little joke, a how do you do, a nod, a wink, a hello is part of the everyday happenings on our streets.

If you see someone you know, WOW! Hugs so tight, never mind what it may look like, we just embrace each other soundly.
Take awhile, catch up. Not so busy rushing nowhere, you can still greet a friend.

The old, the weak, the young, the hardened, and everyone in between, these are the wonderful people of my "Beloved Tenderloin."

It doesn't have to be a Sunday to say a prayer, take time to meditate or bless another. You can pause to enjoy the sunshine or look up and feel the rain on your face. These are the simple wonders to enjoy in the Tenderloin. You can say thank-you for the flower growing around the corner, a blooming shrub, a fragile tree. To me they all say thank you for being alive on what some may consider cold mean streets.

Am I ignoring the fact that there are no bathrooms for the people, "paying customers only," no public bathrooms as there are in other parts of San Francisco. No stores or gas stations that anyone can use to pee. People have nowhere but the sidewalks to exist.

The people try to sleep in a doorway, on a corner, on a piece of cardboard, under a dirty blanket. They close their eyes when they can for a moment, an hour or two. Any longer, and they risk being robbed, arrested or worse.

Some find a few things to sell, to trade, to barter for a hamburger, fries, a coke, a joint, a smoke. You can get a cigarette at the corner store for a quarter. These are the daily acts of existence.

Yes, there are those who terrorize, steal, stab, shoot, violate and constantly threaten violence. I can't explain these acts away. This is not my "Beloved Tenderloin" but it is a reflection of our society from corporate greed to sexual perversity. Our society can be cruel and evil, so let's not pretend this stuff only goes on here in "My Beloved Tenderloin."

It's amazing to me that the worst acting street person can turn around and help someone in trouble. We as a society often ignore those in trouble or pretend nothing is happening, that the person in trouble doesn't exist.

Respect for one another only requires a hand shake, an acknowledging nod, a smile, just simply recognizing each other. More important is the acceptance of someone who is different from you. Diversity in all its beauty and bountifulness is all around us in the Tenderloin. Asians, Blacks, Latinos, Whites, Gays, Straights, Bisexuals, Transgenders live together in this concentrated neighborhood. Those who have handicaps, mental illness, serious addictions all reside here. I often see them coexisting, even accepting each other.

We don't have the luxury of ignoring each other; all our foibles are out there for everyone to see. We can't hide behind closed doors. We also live with those desperate to feed their addictions, not caring how or with what they get their fix. They live their life in a trance, their overwhelming neediness out there 24/7 for all to see. A dose, a fix, a drink helps them put off the pain of living for a little while. This too is a part of "My Beloved Tenderloin."

And then there are the police who have lost their way. They harass those with nothing and nowhere to go. They question the dark skinned people. They treat them like the worst criminals because they are poor, homeless, dirty, sick, marginalized. They arrest them and fine them only to turn them loose back into the streets of the Tenderloin. The never ending downward spiral continues.

I've witnessed the police making snide, disparaging remarks. Telling those of so little that they are bad because they have nothing. It doesn't seem as though the police are able to see real human beings. They often express contempt. Can't they try to see the child who has been neglected, abused, discarded, raped and violated?

The cops get paid to police the "Worst Neighborhood in San Francisco, My Beloved Tenderloin," which is home to many low income families. They live in tiny, cramped one room apartments. Caring for their children and even elderly parents.

The police have an unintended legacy here. They are feared and maligned because of their contemptuous attitudes. My friend says this is probably the only way they can survive.

I wish it were possible for them to look at the people with empathy and to see themselves in service to the poor and the homeless. I wish they could use common courtesy and respect for those who are barely existing. What would it be like to look at the people's faces and give them a sincere smile, an attitude of concern? I wish they could treat our people as human beings worthy of respect. Get to know them as individuals with their own souls however hidden from view.

I have been fortunate to be part of another way in "My Beloved Tenderloin." It's a way of presence, a way of love. Taking time to meditate, reflect, to be aware of my prejudice, look at my own faults and short-comings and take all this into the streets amongst the people of "My Beloved Tenderloin," in The Land of the Living Dead who I love with all my heart.

To All the Fools

NORMAN DEPOVER

Hi Fools,
What can I say? I'm
Following my dream
And keeping alive
My dreams in the head.
What was impossible
Has come possible, I'm
On a journey of life
I'm the most happy that
I've ever been; I have
A good friend (Amber)
& new housing to
look forward to.

Death and Resurrection
—The Rhythm of Nature

Ray Valdez

Would you, capitalist class
pay me, your sworn enemy,
the honor of assassinating me,
as a dangerous, defiant poet?
As you have assassinated
Martin Luther King,
Malcolm X,
Che Guevara,
and maybe Jesus Christ,
gods of Resurrection,
fulminant fertility,
eclipsing winter's vacuity...

Mother's full breast
infusing warm milk:
baby's mouth encircling golden areola,
golden light of solstice, a crowning nimbus ...

fiery veins and arteries
Foliating
oceanic floating, feeling
cosmic connection
of Madonna and Christ,
of Demeter and Persephone,
of Isis and Osiris ...

                I can't think of a better thing to
                          die for than

the cause of Leon Trotsky's humanitarianism,
Leon Trotsky's socialism, for Garcia Lorca's
lyricism, for Pablo Neruda's, for Dylan Thomas,
for John Coltrane, for Langston Hughes ...

Of Mater,
    Matrix
flooding the cosmic spectrum
with galactic milk of kindness, compassion
yes, overflowing,
    inundating death:
the Mother, Tree erect,
with a thousand breasts
who feeds the fury of desire,
the hunger of the soul
for the nutrients of love;
Christ offers the Eucharist
of his blood and body,
as Adonis
    Osiris
        resurrect
the incunabula of eternal return
the fire and heat of passion
over the withering bones
of false Beatitudes
false ideas...

    Yes I write of florets and dewdrops,

but I also write of Blood and Bone ...

Christ—Adonis—Baal—Osiris
gives our daily Beatitude
our resurrected Sun
our cosmic cycle of life
overcoming death;
Christ—Osiris
drinks the milk of the mother goddess;
she presses her body to his lips
her breast expressing
    Love and Heat:
a caloric count for the supernal soul
discovering, creating
the beauty of Earth and Sky.

A Candle in a Glass

Melissa McNeil

I AM ON MY WAY TO MY GRANDMOTHER'S. THE MOON HAS GONE
into hiding, so for light I have only my candle in a glass. I
am wearing my long wooly skirt and my boots of jean
as proof against the cold. The path winds through outcroppings of rock.
When it reaches a grove of old growth trees, my footsteps seem to awaken
the little forest. The air vibrates
with the sounds of wildlife. I drop to the path to listen. There
is the call of the loon from the lake, the screeching of the
bobcats in the bushes, a chorus of whistles and cries
everywhere with their echoes. An owl hoots when it leaves
a branch to perch on a warning sign forbidding trespass. I
arise to go on. All of a sudden the darkness becomes more
intense. A raven has spread its wings overhead. They say it
is bad luck to encounter a raven at midnight. But I am
not afraid, for yonder through yew trees I see my grandmother's
house. Every window lit and she's standing in the doorway
with a lantern in her hand to welcome me, her granddaughter
with a candle in a glass.

A Gift for All

James Zealous

Speaking of gift giving—
and forget about the man who has everything—
what do you give ... the-energy-that-is-everything? ...

is it even possible, this—would it look like ... this—?

MY GIFT TO CREATION: ...
(with full disclosure here folks—
 I may need your help with this)
would be:
simply—
every man, woman, and child
(humanity)
experiencing differently.
let's say, in harmony
with three basic, physical laws supporting this ... shared experience
(reality)

Ready? ...

One: the experience you give, is, the experience you get.
and I'm not telling you anything new
and we already know this shi_t—

if the body of humanity had people ... as cells—
could you know your effect on others?
and how could you tell?

"do unto others as you would have them do unto you—"
is a rule, and a law, and even more—it feels true

And "what goes around comes around?" …

OK—
Two:
the thought that you hold (the good work of the mind)
over time if charged with emotion—the positive, the sublime
when supported by action—not contemplation of belly button
that thought, then …
forms …
comes …
… becomes the thing in the room with you.

And don't we say that
"Dreams Come True"
Well, don't we?

Three:
As your experience can look like the experience you give—
we may see the value of "live and let live"

Know that forgiveness
is … a selfish act— OK?
just know that—
and do it anyway

and if I had but the tiniest grain of wisdom—
i would hold to these three—my templates of sanity
make decisions accordingly
and my only fear would be—
that i may stray from them

decision after decision after decision … the gift is given

Chapter 8

Arise from the Broken

Charles Curtis Blackwell

Lover inside of me come out
With hands raised high
As if to give praise
To the lovely
Shouts and groans
Sing until the sky is undone
Holding up banners, with stains
From tears
Sought in fury of love in sorrow
Here is where I lingered
For so long
Until dirt became clay
Dry and hard
Liken unto my heart
Beaten by life's unfair gains
Now being rained on
I continue to linger here
Bathing in water
God's mercy within
Holding me fast
I grasp all of it

You Choose War

Tony Tepper

You choose war.
My seven-month old daughter
Knows neither right nor wrong.
She is pure.
Wordless, she'll scream
From a fever
But without the dream.
Gurgle, trill, cough
She cannot volunteer,
Say "no" or "yes,"
Identify shrapnel, or
Think we are blessed.

Offer your son
To the country of belief,
To the unheralded thief,
To shards which pierce.
I am afraid
For my daughter and myself.
I am afraid I won't have work.
I am afraid of what we might lose.
I cannot afford
The bravery of your words, the
Blitheness with which
You'd let my daughter slay
An infinite enemy, or be slain.

Blue Tenderloin Kwazy Kat Zen

Ed Bowers

I'm a falling leaf doing kwazy kat zen,
sitting flat on his slats in a Tenderloin Zendo—
234 Hyde St., San Francisco, CA.
Outside this Buddha Lounge,
garbage dogs smoke cracked out hamburger helper
mixed with neurological napalm.
They sit with me as ghostly spirits. I can feel them thinking.
Their astral bodies stretch out cigarette butt fungus fingers for a long lost helping hand
that bows in respect to despair.
Their faces of light
reflect in a mirror full of wisdom
the grief outside this Zendo.
Light has created them to be seen. Do not be deceived by their surface.
They live as light lives when it is honest and it has no choice. They are holy.
They are crucified anonymously in the Greatest Story That Will Never Be Told.
Bow to their invisibility. Their light is now and its meaning is to be seen.
I sit with their holy ghost but their bodies remain outside the Zendo! Why?
There is nothing to be ashamed of here.
This is your mind. Come in and own it! There is a line of nothingness that leads to the
door. Bring it with you.
Transform it into the emptiness of a bird's body.
You too can fly. Your fuel is the shit you sit on that you bring through the door.
Come inside and plant your seeds of destruction in silence.
Silence turns winter into spring! A falling rock sitting in silence becomes a bird
singing in the sky. Try sitting with me. I'm lonely. I will always be alone, but my
aloneness is lonely for you. Let us acknowledge that we will always be alone together
and sit with it.
Citizens of San Francisco! I'm panhandling you! Can you spare an hour to sit with me

in the Zendo at 234 Hyde St. from 9 a.m. to 10 a.m.? Is your time so valuable that you will ignore the infinite silence of no judgment, the finger paints inside the space of your psychedelic mind, the essence of your tormented soul?
I do not deserve to sit alone. I am not that unique.
Explore your mind and I will explore mine. And together, doing this, it will make a third consciousness, a mystery person, the one you are waiting for, perhaps.
At any rate, a little meditation won't hurt. One hour of silence. That's all.
It's funny how a little silence can sometimes save your life.
Sit with me.
Soon.

We Come from the Sun

Lynett Durgin

We come from the sun and worship the sun.
It's there that I see my reflection.
Each morning I align my inner eye with the sun
and there I AM.

A beautiful, glorious purple light being,
surrounded by blue orbs.
Mentally, I grasp my translucent crimson sword
which summers in the light above me
As I draw in my golden halo above me,
I watch as the pieces form a perfect circle.

As I look through the veil that
surrounds our planet, I feel the energy
of the stars join me. The energy of love and
light fills my aura and I hear the sweet hum
of the universe

As I breathe in the sun's energy, I dream of my home
among the stars where the light shines in brilliant
hues of green and blue and violet.

As the stars enfold me, I see a large winnowing
snake of black and silver which calls to mind the
patterns of the Void.

Translucent circles of light engulf me.
And soon I feel the heartbeat of my loved one
join me—so close yet so far.

We are spirit and we are form.

I gaze into the sun and see my reflection.
Yet it is the earthly love that fuels
my swollen heart.

I worship this love with my mate who draws me
close in with warm, strong, loving arms.
We start our night's journey sitting
by the fire on the beach.
Half asleep we move to the cave as the
                    wind comes up.
Soon the sound of waves breaking and
                    wind blowing outside our
refuge awakens us. Our bellies still full
we share the peace of our bodies huddled
together worn from engaging the waves.
We share ourselves and traverse the
                    dimensions
in ecstasy so that we no longer feel our third
dimensional
selves. We rise in our ecstasy ever
higher and higher until in our crescendo
                    of love
we fall back down to earth drained yet
                    transformed.
We are one with all that is.

You're not saying Billy has died …

Kathrin Kapp

You're not saying Billy has died
With the sun bleached hair
With the generous smile?
You're not saying his sickness has zapped the
Last out of him
The last of his health
The last of his will?
You're not saying Billy has died
Who gave up so many times
And then stood up again?
Billy with the shopping cart
Billy with all pain Billy
And shrug and look away

I heard he may have just left town
Moved to another state
Let's hope that he has found a place
Where he can get strong again!
No you're not saying Billy has died
With the sadness in his heart
With the questions in his eyes
You're not saying he is no more
—Billy whom I brought some soup
When he was too weak to walk
Who would cry and cry
But then suddenly smile
Spread out his arms in the mild sunshine

You're not saying Billy has died
—He must have moved away
—I heard he had been talking about leaving
He may have found some peace somewhere out there
So let us now, let us, instead of grieving
Pray that he has found happiness somewhere!

In the rain

Dan Brady

In the rain
Everything is touched
Whether it will or not,
Likes or dislikes

Its clarity
Reflects everything—
Bends all the light
Through its dropped lens

Catches the sun
In points
Which depend from branch or stem

It runs along
On everything
And cleans
Gleans
Glistens and
Wrinkled … in streams
It gleams

Colored transparent
It has no viewpoint
Or every viewpoint
It has no location
Or every location

In the rain
We are all wet
No blessings are withheld
None are excepted from its care
Anyone can enjoy its freedom
To give
Everything to everyone
Endlessly providing
The wonder and grace of love!

For the Blind Woman that Read Red

Vincent Kobelt

We roll her to the stage
Lower the microphone to her mouth
Silence be rolling before she speaks
Silence be honey
Oozing like o's from oolong
And her mouth is still as a stone
And then her hand reaches for the page
Making it keloid and
                          She touching the keloids
                                  with her fingers.

She speaks
Her words curl and swirl into our ears
And dive into our minds.

These words love to be spoken by her
They ripple through the stones of our minds.
She could read the color red if she wanted to.

"Can you listen to the jewel in your chest?" she says.

It is a certain light that makes it glimmer
and the blind woman provided that light today.

July 30, 2007

Jeanne Bryan

Full moon, you let your curtains down.
Often I cannot see you in the mist
and you know that few places
in San Francisco stars are visible.

In the Middle East there are many stars
and I have heard there was once One Star.
How many murders since.
Tonight the full moon is in Iraq,
It is in Iran, it shines over Israel.

Full moon, golden and white,
you are a liar.
You make lovely our suburbs and our deserts,
our mountains and our plains.
The stars gather in pictures.

Do the young in Baghdad look at the stars
and read fortunes?
Full moon, you look at corpses. I don't
understand the sense of wars,
the protocol, but I know the same moon

that I can't see well is full tonight and then
again, Jeannie, you are wrong. Half a world
away the moon has set, it is dark.

Excerpt #43: From File Clerk at Allianz

Mel C. Thompson

The file clerk as self-effacing existentialist
reading Camus alone in a corner on breaks.
He hasn't had a real date in several years.

The file clerk as guilt-ridden former Catholic
unable to masturbate due to subconscious guilt.
He failed his first class in human sexuality.

The file clerk as creepy Libertarian with
a Ron Paul button on his lapel, eating whole
pizzas for dinner with six packs of soda.

The file clerk as former liberal-turned-
born-again-Christian who still smokes pot
and tries hard to convert UPS drivers.

The file clerk as would-be gospel singer
who can't carry a tune and whose car rattles
as though it were dying of emphysema.

The file clerk as failed applicant for all
branches of the military and all police forces.
He is studying civil service exam books.

The file clerk as acne-ridden patriot
sporting a flag pin on his polyester lapel.
They haven't the heart to try to fire him.

The file clerk as pseudo-intellectual
and speed reader who remembers nothing.
He has just become an Amway distributor.

The file clerk as rabid conspiracy theorist
who frequents Philippine psychic surgeons.
Please keep the file clerk in your prayers.

Ride the Tiger

J.R. Johnson

Oh leave me cheap despondency you and
Your surly crew, too long I suffered your
Insolence never will I return to you, all
The insults and accusations, the put downs
For which I hate you, begone to the error
From which you came, I've scaled the wall
To safety free at last from your horrid
Pit of shame

Providence heard my pitiful cries gave
Me passage to the world of light. These were
Eyes in Phantom clothing offering license
To the boldest. This anxious candidate
Readily took his leave

Stumbled across the tasseled shag of comely
Shape and smartly dressed, complete with
Rippled coat petitions, apt virtues for
The newly ambitious expressing courage
Of a heroic propensity, I mounted this
Steed with unswerving confidence.

Tiger, tiger, tiger, fly me to exhilaration
To entertainment, to fantasies and extravaganzas.
Faster tiger Faster. Show me
Johannesburg, Paris, and the Broadways

Faster tiger faster, take me to the
Center of Ova's Basket.

Closer tiger closer, to wrap my
Mind in Dame Fortune's music

Tiger, tiger, tiger, light, light, light,
Grip the tassel tight,
Off we go, hang tight,
Feel the heat.

Fear

Mark Morris

I see you suffer
I watch while you bleed
you'll never see how much it hurts me
I hate what's hurting you
we've been traveling this Earth forever
the hands of time have slapped our faces
I cry while they steal you away
they start with your fingertips and then
they reach for your heart
now they are stealing us blind
tearing us apart
you can barely see
I cry while you fade away
you have taken me from sea to shining sea
together we found Paradise
the coldest winter shined like the brightest
diamond when you were here
I shed another icy tear
while you dwindle away
for you I feel aching fear
or is the fear for me?
will I be the next one taken?

Poem for the Ministry

Nahshon Chapman

WE ALL ARE INFINITE NEBULA
BROUGHT INTO THIS WORLD
SOME SHINE BRIGHTER THAN
OTHERS BUT WHEN YOU SHINE
UPON A PRISON YOU TRULY ARE
AN APEX BEACON OF LIGHT

Mind the Pain
(a look at pre-post death in the face)

RICARDO LUNA

The gentrification of calamity
hooded stocking ten feet tall
your hooded treasure
of yielding surprise

last of rock bottom she'd surrender
look i'm still in bed
arching reaching
finding my memory
standing ten feet tall

the empty heart empty hand
clearly understood savior nowhere
my wedding bells
still ring in my mind

treason asunder my love dispatched
i a regret
some solace the mystery
of your heaven spent
a little too true
dying in mine

the love theatrics are perfect and more
their mine til eternal
how girl
you are
ten feet tall

who are you leaving behind
will you change what you come back to
will you contribute and share
so others don't have
to go there

gotta guide to take you there
here
and everywhere

City Shaman

Marcus Colasurdo

If you look closely (with your third eye)
   you can see him walking
alone in attic clothing
through the swarmed
bandaged streets.
Any city.
     Any time.
He's clicking a hand carved
    totem stick
in a third-legged rhythm—
on his way anywhere
   to riddle the sphinx
        into   laughter.
He lights up frankincense
    and hands out poems on blasted
streetcorners.
He carries aloe
    and cayenne
and a harmonica
in his plastic bag medicine pouch.
The ziggurats of the cash district
  cast no shadow upon him.
He sings scat in Ur tongues
  on the soup kitchen lines.
What he has,
  he gives away:
thus he is invisible to definition.
Sometimes

  only the children can see him
and they cannot explain
their wild glee and fresh fruit
  to questioning adults.
To the naked eye,
   to the passing patrol car,
  to the fashionably late downtown diners,
he seems quite insane
  This notion makes him smile
  and lick the tip of his pencil:
he's got the papers to prove it.

The First Day of Summer

LOUISE SHULTZ

The street was particularly raunchy today—anger and disillusion adding to gray sky and heavy air in the form of loud raucous laughter, some moans—jabber jabber merging with scratchy booming of harsh-toned music breaking the sound barrier like a broken glass.

Then there was an uncomfortable quiet, huddled in blanketed corners. It is as though the ocean air forgot to come to the street today—twisting back to a different neighborhood looking for a more cordial welcome. Yes, today the ocean air has broken its promise to wash the atmosphere clean and blow away the night stench. Tired of its day job—playing hooky from the street.

The street was particularly scary today—the sun missing this first day of Summer with its hopes and dreams and stories of a new day that golden sun rays bring—brilliant like a fresh squeezed juice over ice in a crystal cup.

On the street—groups of men in tatters restlessly—waiting—waiting—waiting for something to happen—some powerful and benevolent force to turn to the next page—to open a new book—to save the day.

A sleeping person—man or woman—sits on the ground overtaken by boredom or exhaustion. Stale beer drips from the bottle he holds loosely— dangles loosely from his scarred hand – soon to shatter on the cracked sidewalk and disrupt the rhythm of steady snores and lazy footsteps on the pavement.

Still amid the grayness, always peeks a smile, a sweet hello from the girl behind a purple wig, or kind gaze from the old man moving slowly down the sidewalk propped up in a worn wheelchair. Or a sweet hello—from a soft-eyed elderly

woman, a brown winter coat wrapped around her thin body—a sincere request for just some change. She willingly shares a look—eye to eye. There are always those proud souls who remain resilient or just lucky, refusing to be sucked dry by poverty, hunger, or by the loneliness of a gray day—a
disappointing first day of Summer.

Perhaps on this day the Mighty One or Ones took a chance and threw us a curve— inviting us to light up the world with shining iridescent promises and to spread them far and wide—miles beyond our self-drawn boundaries— spraying our light like huge graffiti messages along the street; on this
particularly raunchy somewhat scary Summer day …

A challenge to be bigger—a dare—an extra-credit assignment.

Maybe even an expectation—to spread our light with greater force, more directly, more willingly, and more kindly on this gray First Day of Summer.

Once upon an unlimited EBT card ...

Mike Stone

Little girls dream of becoming princesses ... Little boys dream of becoming pro football players... **I just dream of having an unlimited EBT card ... (Well, okay...** just for one day!)

As a near-homeless person (God Bless the SRO Hotel Program!), I am always running out of credit on my EBT card long before month-end. Now what do I do!? Horrible visions of standing in long, long lines in front of Glide Methodist Church while "good hard-working San Franciscans" drive past me makes me shudder ... Especially when I think of how they slow down all of a sudden so they can teach their children what can happen to them. The little ones point and giggle ... Sometimes they cry ... But, what can I say; the line is an always-changing variety of endless variations on the theme of human individuality ... Short people, tall people, **neat** people, *grungy people*, bizarre, scary, disturbed, and peacefully pleasant—people, all in line waiting to get something to **eat**.

So, as I stood there gazing up at the shiny, gleaming tower of wealth across the street, better known as **the San Francisco Hilton,** I started to daydream ... What if I had a day of unlimited credit on my EBT card? What would that be like? ...

Picture it ... I'm up bright and early on a very sun-shiny morning and I'm off to shop at Safeway and I say—**shop like I mean it ...**

I stroll in and pull my shopping cart out of the group with confidence. I glide over to the prepared food section and I pick up a prepackaged "7 layer dip (complete with tostada chips)." Let's see, ... I'll also need two or three packages of hot wings with ranch dipping sauce for an appetizer before dinner ... and one or two bottles of Jones Blue Bubblegum soda pop ... (I ignore the disapproving glances of all the "proper" housewives who, of course, don't approve of such rich food in the middle of the day!)

And then, ... it's over to the "serve yourself" salad bar where I begin to pick up a giant sized carton to fill with fresh spinach leaves. As I ponder over the vast selection of fresh veggies, cheeses, and fruit, I begin to think about the salad dressing selections ...

Suddenly, a rather large and unfriendly woman shoves me towards the cottage cheese and says ...

"I know you! You have one of those EBT cards, don't you! Do you think it's **wise** to be so frivolous with such **limited** resources? ...?

"Well!," I say ... "I guess you don't worry about not having enough to eat ... You're a virtual **'horn-of-plenty'** when it comes to reserves!"

... **AND THEN** ... I defiantly pick up a huge piece of chocolate fudge cake aud a can of reddi-whip ... "Is that for a midnight snack?", she quips ... I DON'T DO WHIPPED CREAM PARTIES LADY!   Of course not ...

I begin eyeing a tray of succulent deviled eggs as she turns, clicks on her shiny paten leather heels, and storms away. A brief, but *"powerfully moving"* wave of guilt comes over me and I decide against them. But—I do grab three or four jars of Ruffles Brand French Onion dip and Nacho Cheese dip on the way to the register. All of a sudden, I
remember that CALA-Bell Foods sells "Krispy Kreme" donuts!!! I'll need at least two dozen, I think, and I keep thinking of endless possibilities as the checker tallies up my bill and packs up my groceries.

On the way over to CALA-Bell, I begin to think about something else really extravagant—One of those delicious meatball subs from Subway. Only, not the usual "once-a-month" six-inch special—I WANT THE WHOLE ENCHILADA!!! A fully loaded 12 inch meatball sub with extra cheese, meatballs and sauce with three not one packages of chips— *(A real indulgence)*

Later that afternoon, I struggle up the stairs with all that luscious food and my EBT card balance still intact. As I settled onto the bed to watch the evening news, chow down on my meatball sub, and ponder dessert and coffee, I think to myself—"What a day! What a city! **Such a deal! ..."**

A Life on Purpose

Fran Cesarone

How she loved to make collage.

In fact, one might say that was her purpose in life. While she slept, she perceived a slideshow of images which she was compelled to recreate in the tangible world of her work.

The collages had magnificent diversity. Some were as small as a thumbnail; others so large, they were visible from outer space, just like the Great Wall of China. She loved mixing media and often surprised herself by integrating a smorgasbord of materials. Some collages were two-dimensional while others had a depth so penetrating, it was impossible to walk past the creations without making physical contact. The instant of contact was profound. It was not unusual to feel as if the art itself were alive; merging evoked tremendous emotions and triggered intense memories. She did not strive to rouse these reactions. She simply created, incorporating elements magnetized through her soul.

Others desired to know her. She smiled, for there was no better way to come to know her than through her art. She delighted in witnessing others interacting with her creations. When she saw them illuminate, weep, anger, tremble, and soften, she knew her path was right. It was intended.

When she died, she was enveloped by her creations and merged with them. There was no separation. A flame was lit, and the energy of the glorious blaze was a testament to who she was: one who lived her life on purpose.

Retired

Jason Hy

Coffee shop,
comfortable chair,
knees at the picture window,
coffee on table at my side,
bag lunch,
almond butter
on whole grain bread.

Pleasant out,
wide sidewalk,
filled with people,
no end to them,
a unique life
sculpted in each face.

Nothing to do
next three hours.
This is a good place.
I'll stay here.
Read.
Look at passers-by.
Nothing to do.

News on a March Full Moon

David Plumb

Somewhere in a nearby yard a blue jay
yaks and yaks the morning quiet
way beyond the clicking news of smiles
and banks washing profits off casket walls.
Mid morning and the news reads
Sarandrea, Jessica Y., 22, Pfc, Army; Miami
First Cavalry Divison. Killed in Iraq.

Marjorie Pollock is text messaging
by the organic oranges at Whole Foods.
Neal Bellenger holds a two pound
ground buffalo package in his left hand
a cell phone in his right.
The newlyweds contemplate organic cane
sugar as second ingredients in yogurt.
Daniel B. Hyde, 24 First Lieutenant, Army,
Modesto, California is dead in Iraq.

Beyond the three dollar collard greens
traffic zips and tears the afternoon.
No need to signal or cut off the competition.
It's only three lanes and four hundred yards
to the gas station and a cheap hoagie.
A homeless man passes out a newspaper
at the traffic island. Put a little in the pot
please, and God Bless you. Jeffrey Reed, 23,
Army Sergeant, Chesterfield, Virginia dead in Iraq.

Late afternoon stuffs the mind, wipes

pleasure off a job that may or may not
exist in a few days, or tomorrow.
Lorna Guzman, social worker for Women
in Distress hopes Day Care is taking care.
Keisha wants to tell the M.D.
with 40 patients a day that
she missed another period.
She has to get home.
She has a class tonight.
Patrick De Voe, he's dead in Afghanistan
Twenty-seven, Private First Class
from Auburn, New York.
You know where that is, but then
It's almost dinner time and Shirley
brings in take out hot and sour, lo mein
a side of barbecued wings.
Did you hear Tiger's back?
TVs blink the news, the news, the news.
Who did what and who said if?
She's a Democrat underneath.
How about that short horse in England?
They think it's stuck in mud.
George Clooney may show up on ER.
You know Rush Lim and the other one
who took all the rich guy's cash.
He's going to plead and Jay Leno
will have his say later on.

By the way, it's a full moon.
Look out the window at the perfect sky but
don't forget the names whispered in the stars.
Jessica, Daniel, Jeffrey, Patrick
echo in blood, in guns, in storms.
They're coming home.

The Day of Darkness

Belle Starr

There was a time a lady in green found her day to feel dark and serene.
As she went about her daily work, she discovered the ilk of the ire.
She felt her will, her heart, her desire.
Slipping away it felt to she; as though someone were stealing it, the joy, the glee.
The woman we know as our beloved Rhiannon knew not what to do, didn't know what was the matter.
Things seemed more than out of place for she. In whatever way, she knew not why, "why must it be?"
"Perhaps it is a dream, and I shall wake soon," she said. She was so tired, and ready for bed.
As she lay her head down on the pillow that night, she still did fret, she still did plight. But reserved herself to a dream of knowledge to find out the matter to prevent any blockage.
As she fell in slumber, she woke in her dream, in the darkest cavern all in dark green. Vines and root surrounded her everywhere.
She knew not what to do, but decided to explore. She soon discovered that she was deep in the earth, she knew not how or how she got there.
But she knew that somehow, there was a meaning, she must now draw.
Carefully, she looked around, and soon found a shovel, she picked it up and begin to dig and toil. She worked for what seems like a week, to dig a large hole, to dig it deep.
Then she found many of her clothes and things dropped them in the hole, and began to sing. She knew not the whole meaning, until again;
She glanced back in the hole, and understood it all in an instant, just then.
The clothes and things were not clothes at all, but things she needed to rid herself of once and for all. These things were: despair, depression, and

lament. As soon as she saw them the weight lifted, she no longer felt spent.
As she turned around, the cavern gave way, and was standing in the sunlight of a bright shiny day. She now understood that this hole was a box of one called Pandora, minus the paradox. For things to her were as clear as the air. No longer depression, no longer despair. She now could only see the good and warmth of a bright summer day, and nothing could touch her, and nothing could sway the feeling of joy, serenity and peace surrounded and shone from her, so bright and so sweet.
Rhiannon, my sister, the one of warm light, has a joy and an energy within her, and in very plain sight. She needed the time to put away the nasty things in her life. To rid her of pain and anger and strife.
Even in a dream in an instant and way, we all know that this process will ever come one day. With work and patience, and ever remembering the joy. The sunshine, the warmth, the sweetness, the serenity.
In every way we count our blessings. For strife and pain, and depression leads to good things you'll see. As ever we will, so mote it be!!

INDEX

Aki, RaMu	105		Campbell, Marsha	139
Allen, Dee	86		Carney, Thomas	10
Amun (via Metu)	78		Carol, Utah	120
Atlantis	66		Cesarone, Fran	216
Bayliss, Nell	-		Chapman, Nahshon	207
Belz, Paul	30		Clarke, Jess (Ben)	168
Bindhill, Michelle	65		Clifford, Bob	37
Blackwell, Charles Curtis	190		Cimprich, Vickie	130
Boesing, Martha	95		Colasurdo, Marcus	2010
Bolstridge, Gary	90		Curo, Forrest	48
Booker, Bob	6		Davidson, Ethan	108
Bowden, William	111		Davis, Garland	22
Bowers, Ed	v, 192		Delaney, John	118
Brady, Dan	198		Dennison, Sam	i
Breiger, Marek	75		DePover, Norman	181
Brennan, Don	125		Dorbin, Sanford	131
Brown, Taylor	128		Drabkin, Paul	165
Bryan, Jeanne	201		Dranow, Ralph	88
Calin, Denis	148		Duke, John	134

Dunkle, Owen	94	JoJo	136
Durgin, Lynett	194	Kandinsky, Carla	36
Evans, Deirdre	144	Kapp, Kathrin	196
Fallon, Joel	113	Karnazes, Zach	126
Fingland, Randy	3	Kazalia, Marie	2
Ford, Gail	60	Khattab, Debra Grace	34
Gallagher, Clyde	68	Knutson, Susan	58
Ganz, Mary	23	Kobelt, Vincent	200
Gonzales, Bernardo	50	Kominars, Sheppard Benet	162
Greene, Meg Whittaker	171	Krieger, Kat	176
Hayes, T.	72	Kuhwald, Kurt	29
Hirschman, Jack	147	Loonin, Alexandra	92
Hoodlum, R.	104	o.d. ludyeh (Bernie Sullivan)	152
Hy, Jason	217	Lumpkin, Kirk	18
Jacqui	135	Luna, Ricardo	208
Jensen, Dale	49	Mann, Joshua	80
Joesph Jr., Jeffery Jewelle	174	Marlin, Daniel	45
Johnson, J.R.	204	Marlin, Jeffery	82
Johnson, Jesse James	98	McNeil, Melissa	185

Mercer, Bill	62	qrhandjr	156
Michaels, J.	161	Rainwater, Gloria	138
Miloradovich, Alex	38	Rashna	57
Milstein, Norm	110	Ratch, Jerry	172
Moconnor	76	Reed, Zack	173
Moe, H.D.	116	Rennon	54
Moon, Janell	140	Rhodes, John	59
Morris, Mark	206	Roams, Dave	155
Murphy, David T.	77	Robbins, David	19
Murphy, Garrett	114	Robertson, Eric	11
Mycue, Edward	31	Rudge, Mary	44
Nails, Phillip T.	8	Sauer, Ronald F.	167
Nakayama, Delia Tomino	143	Savage, Keith	56
Newman, Melissa	112	Schooley, David	166
Niemczyk, Mike	81	Sears, Anna	146
Nordkwelle, Mary	84	Sher, David	42
Odegard, Tom	149	Shultz, Louise	212
Plumb, David	218	Small, Fay	145
Pogorelov, Vlad	15	Smith, Robert Lavett	39

Starr, Belle	220	Wilson, Nancy	40
Steckel, Jan	123	Wolf, Matt	89
Stone, Mike	214	Wright, Yolanda	83
Tepper, Tony	191	Wynn, George	150
Thompsen, Sara	69	Zealous, James	186
Thompson, Mel C.	202	Zeftel, Mitchell	100
Trian, Chris	24		
Tucker, M.A.	28		
Turchin, Gary	14		
Turi, Alfred	64		
Turner, Debra	119		
Valdez, Ray	182		
Vianey	32		
Vinograd, Julia	63		
Walker, Patricia	4		
Walker, Keith	124		
Warren	160		
Wells, Judy	74		
Whittaker, Diamond Dave	122		

www.ingramcontent.com/pod-product-compliance
Lightning Source LLC
Chambersburg PA
CBHW080440170426
43195CB00017B/2830